Visual Factfinder

WORLD HISTORY

Visual Factfinder
WORLD HISTORY

KEN HILLS

Kingfisher Books

NEW YORK

KINGFISHER BOOKS
Grisewood & Dempsey Inc.
95 Madison Avenue
New York, New York 10016

First American edition 1993

2 4 6 8 10 9 7 5 3 1 (lib. bdg.)
2 4 6 8 10 9 7 5 3 1 (pbk.)

Library of Congress Cataloging-in-Publication Data
Hills, Ken.
World history/Ken Hills.—1st American ed.
p. cm.—(The Kingfisher visual factfinder)
Includes index.
Summary: Surveys world history, from early civilizations
to the birth of new nations in modern times.
1. World history—Pictorial works—Juvenile literature.
2. World history—Juvenile literature.
[1. World history.] I. Title.
II. Series: Visual factfinders.
D21.1.H46   1993
909—dc20   93-20105   CIP   AC

ISBN 1-85697-854-0 (lib. bdg.)
ISBN 1-85697-853-2 (pbk.)

Series Editor: Michèle Byam
Assistant Editor: Cynthia O'Neill
Series Designer: Ralph Pitchford
Designers: Shaun Barlow, Cathy Tincknell
Picture Research: Elaine Willis, Su Alexander

Additional help from
Martin Wilson, Hilary Bird
Sandra Begnor
Janet Woronkowicz

Printed in Spain

CONTENTS

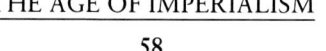

About this Factfinder

This encyclopedic reference book gives essential facts and figures about the most important events and people in the history of the world from prehistoric times to the present age. Each topic is interpreted in a highly visual style with color illustrations, maps, and photographs that complement the text.

A timechart gives quick and easy reference to major historical events and personalities. There are also box features that summarize additional key facts.

Short text essays introduce key periods of world history, including ancient empires and civilizations, the Renaissance, the Age of Discovery and the two world wars.

Clear and colorful maps provide further reference on wars and revolutions, world exploration, individual countries' territorial gains and losses, and social changes.

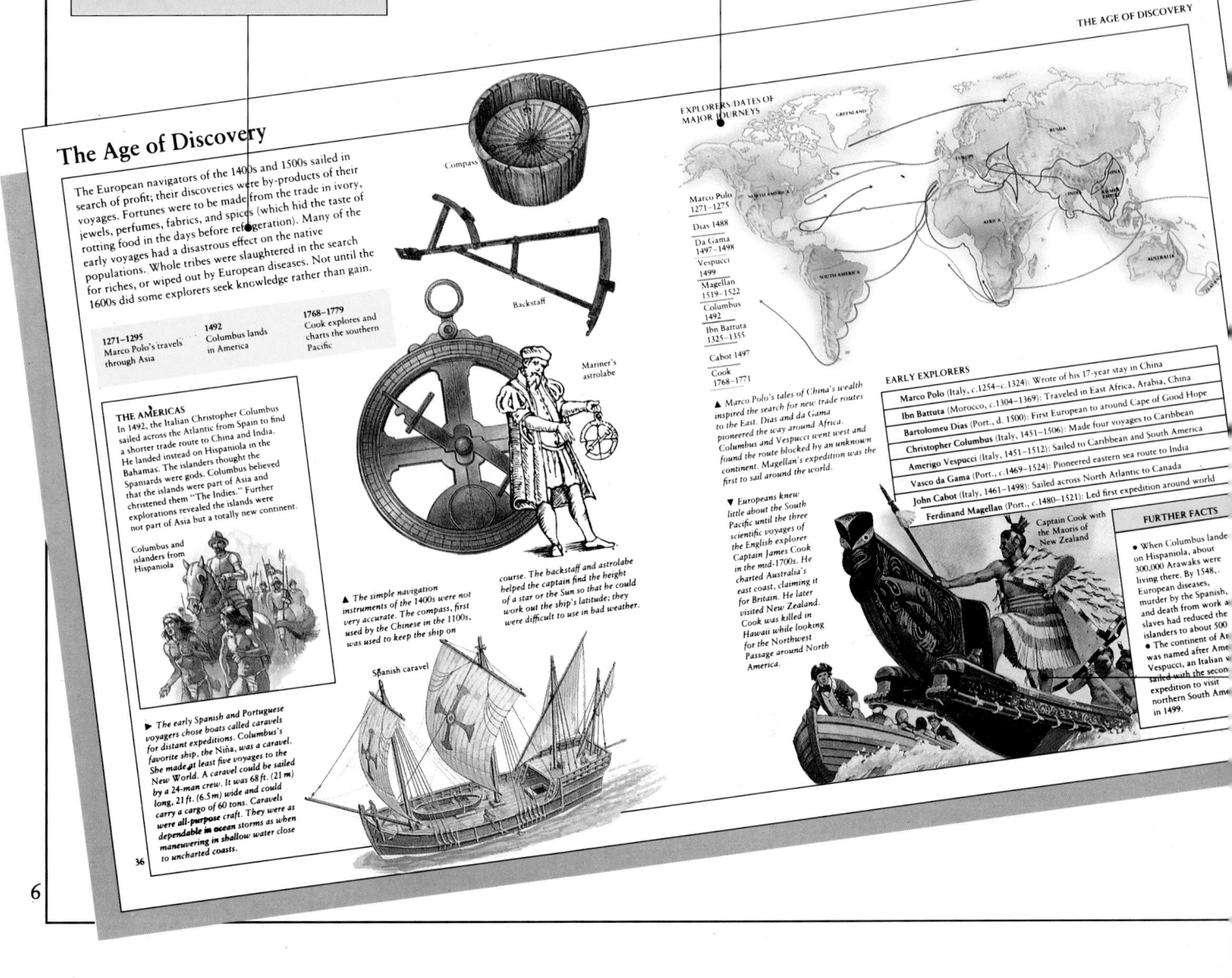

THE AGE OF DISCOVERY

The Age of Discovery

The European navigators of the 1400s and 1500s sailed in search of profit; their discoveries were by-products of their voyages. Fortunes were to be made from the trade in ivory, jewels, perfumes, fabrics, and spices (which hid the taste of rotting food in the days before refrigeration). Many of the early voyages had a disastrous effect on the native populations. Whole tribes were slaughtered in the search for riches, or wiped out by European diseases. Not until the 1600s did some explorers seek knowledge rather than gain.

| 1271–1295 Marco Polo's travels through Asia | 1492 Columbus lands in America | 1768–1779 Cook explores and charts the southern Pacific |

THE AMERICAS
In 1492, the Italian Christopher Columbus sailed across the Atlantic from Spain to find a shorter trade route to China and India. He landed instead on Hispaniola in the Bahamas. The islanders thought the Spaniards were gods. Columbus believed that the islands were part of Asia and christened them "The Indies." Further explorations revealed the islands were not part of Asia but a totally new continent.

Columbus and islanders from Hispaniola

▲ The simple navigation instruments of the 1400s were not very accurate. The compass, first used by the Chinese in the 1100s, was used to keep the ship on course. The backstaff and astrolabe helped the captain find the height of a star or the Sun so that he could work out the ship's latitude; they were difficult to use in bad weather.

Compass

Backstaff

Mariner's astrolabe

Spanish caravel

▶ The early Spanish and Portuguese voyagers chose boats called caravels for distant expeditions. Columbus's favorite ship, the Niña, was a caravel. She made at least five voyages to the New World. A caravel could be sailed by a 24-man crew. It was 68 ft. (21 m) long, 21 ft. (6.5 m) wide and could carry a cargo of 60 tons. Caravels were all-purpose craft. They were as dependable in ocean storms as when maneuvering in shallow water close to uncharted coasts.

36

EXPLORERS' DATES OF MAJOR JOURNEYS

GREENLAND

Marco Polo 1271–1275
Dias 1488
Da Gama 1497–1498
Vespucci 1499
Magellan 1519–1522
Columbus 1492
Ibn Battuta 1325–1355
Cabot 1497
Cook 1768–1771

▲ Marco Polo's tales of China's wealth inspired the search for new trade routes to the East. Dias and da Gama pioneered the way around Africa. Columbus and Vespucci went west and found the route blocked by an unknown continent. Magellan's expedition was the first to sail around the world.

▼ Europeans knew little about the South Pacific until the three scientific voyages of the English explorer Captain James Cook in the mid-1700s. He charted Australia's east coast, claiming it for Britain. He later visited New Zealand. Cook was killed in Hawaii while looking for the Northwest Passage around North America.

EARLY EXPLORERS
| Marco Polo (Italy, c.1254–c.1324): Wrote of his 17-year stay in China |
| Ibn Battuta (Morocco, c.1304–1369): Traveled in East Africa, Arabia, China |
| Bartolomeu Dias (Port., d. 1500): First European to around Cape of Good Hope |
| Christopher Columbus (Italy, 1451–1506): Made four voyages to Caribbean |
| Amerigo Vespucci (Italy, 1451–1512): Sailed to Caribbean and South America |
| Vasco da Gama (Port., c.1469–1524): Pioneered eastern sea route to India |
| John Cabot (Italy, 1461–1498): Sailed across North Atlantic to Canada |
| Ferdinand Magellan (Port., c.1480–1521): Led first expedition around world |

Captain Cook with the Maoris of New Zealand

FURTHER FACTS
• When Columbus landed on Hispaniola, about 300,000 Arawaks were living there. By 1548, European diseases, murder by the Spanish, and death from work as slaves had reduced the islanders to about 500

• The continent of A[...] was named after Ame[...] Vespucci, an Italian w[...] sailed with the secon[...] expedition to visit northern South Ame[...] in 1499.

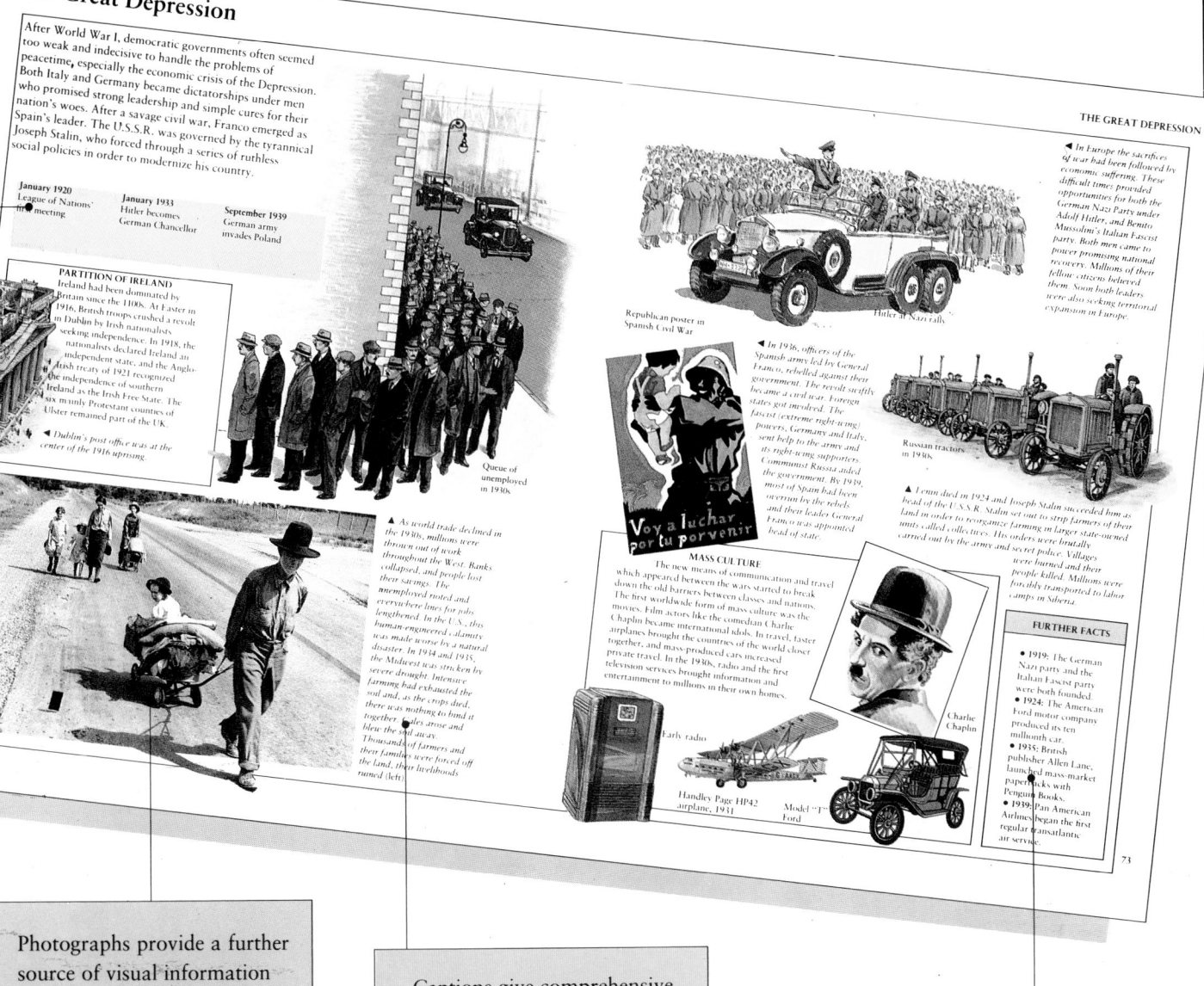

The Great Depression

After World War I, democratic governments often seemed too weak and indecisive to handle the problems of peacetime, especially the economic crisis of the Depression. Both Italy and Germany became dictatorships under men who promised strong leadership and simple cures for their nation's woes. After a savage civil war, Franco emerged as Spain's leader. The U.S.S.R. was governed by the tyrannical Joseph Stalin, who forced through a series of ruthless social policies in order to modernize his country.

January 1920
League of Nations' first meeting

January 1933
Hitler becomes German Chancellor

September 1939
German army invades Poland

PARTITION OF IRELAND
Ireland had been dominated by Britain since the 1100s. At Easter in 1916, British troops crushed a revolt in Dublin by Irish nationalists seeking independence. In 1918, the nationalists declared Ireland an independent state, and the Anglo-Irish treaty of 1921 recognized the independence of southern Ireland as the Irish Free State. The six mainly Protestant counties of Ulster remained part of the UK.

◀ Dublin's post office was at the center of the 1916 uprising.

◀ As world trade declined in the 1930s, millions were thrown out of work throughout the West. Banks collapsed, and people lost their savings. The unemployed noted and everywhere lines for jobs lengthened. In the U.S., this human-engineered calamity was made worse by a natural disaster. In 1934 and 1935, the Midwest was stricken by severe drought. Intensive farming had exhausted the soil and, as the crops died, there was nothing to bind it together. Gales arose and blew the soil away. Thousands of farmers and their families were forced off the land, their livelihoods ruined (left).

Queue of unemployed in 1930s

Republican poster in Spanish Civil War

Hitler at Nazi rally

◀ In Europe the sacrifices of war had been followed by economic suffering. These difficult times provided opportunities for both the German Nazi Party under Adolf Hitler, and Benito Mussolini's Italian Fascist party. Both men came to power promising national recovery. Millions of their fellow citizens believed them. Soon both leaders were also seeking territorial expansion in Europe.

◀ In 1936, officers of the Spanish army led by General Franco, rebelled against their government. The revolt swiftly became a civil war. Foreign states got involved. The fascist (extreme right-wing) powers, Germany and Italy, sent help to the army and its right-wing supporters. Communist Russia aided the government. By 1939, most of Spain had been overrun by the rebels and their leader General Franco was appointed head of state.

Russian tractors in 1930s

◀ Lenin died in 1924 and Joseph Stalin succeeded him as head of the U.S.S.R. Stalin set out to strip farmers of their land in order to reorganize farming in larger state-owned units called collectives. His orders were brutally carried out by the army and secret police. Villages were burned and their people killed. Millions were forcibly transported to labor camps in Siberia.

MASS CULTURE
The new means of communication and travel which appeared between the wars started to break down the old barriers between classes and nations. The first worldwide form of mass culture was the movies. Film actors like the comedian Charlie Chaplin became international idols. In travel, faster airplanes brought the countries of the world closer together, and mass-produced cars increased private travel. In the 1930s, radio and the first television services brought information and entertainment to millions in their own homes.

Charlie Chaplin

Early radio

Handley Page HP42 airplane, 1931

Model "T" Ford

FURTHER FACTS
• 1919: The German Nazi party and the Italian Fascist party were both founded.
• 1924: The American Ford motor company produced its ten millionth car.
• 1935: British publisher Allen Lane launched mass-market paperbacks with Penguin Books.
• 1939: Pan American Airlines began the first regular transatlantic air service.

73

Photographs provide a further source of visual information about the 20th century by showing significant world events such as the Great Depression of the 1930s.

Captions give comprehensive in-depth information on subjects such as the founding of the world's religions, famous battles, great empires, and important social changes.

Quick-reference data boxes provide essential facts and figures on the famous people, major events, and historical movements that have shaped world history.

Detailed illustrations showing scenes from each historical period and every major world civilization help to bring the story of humankind vividly to life.

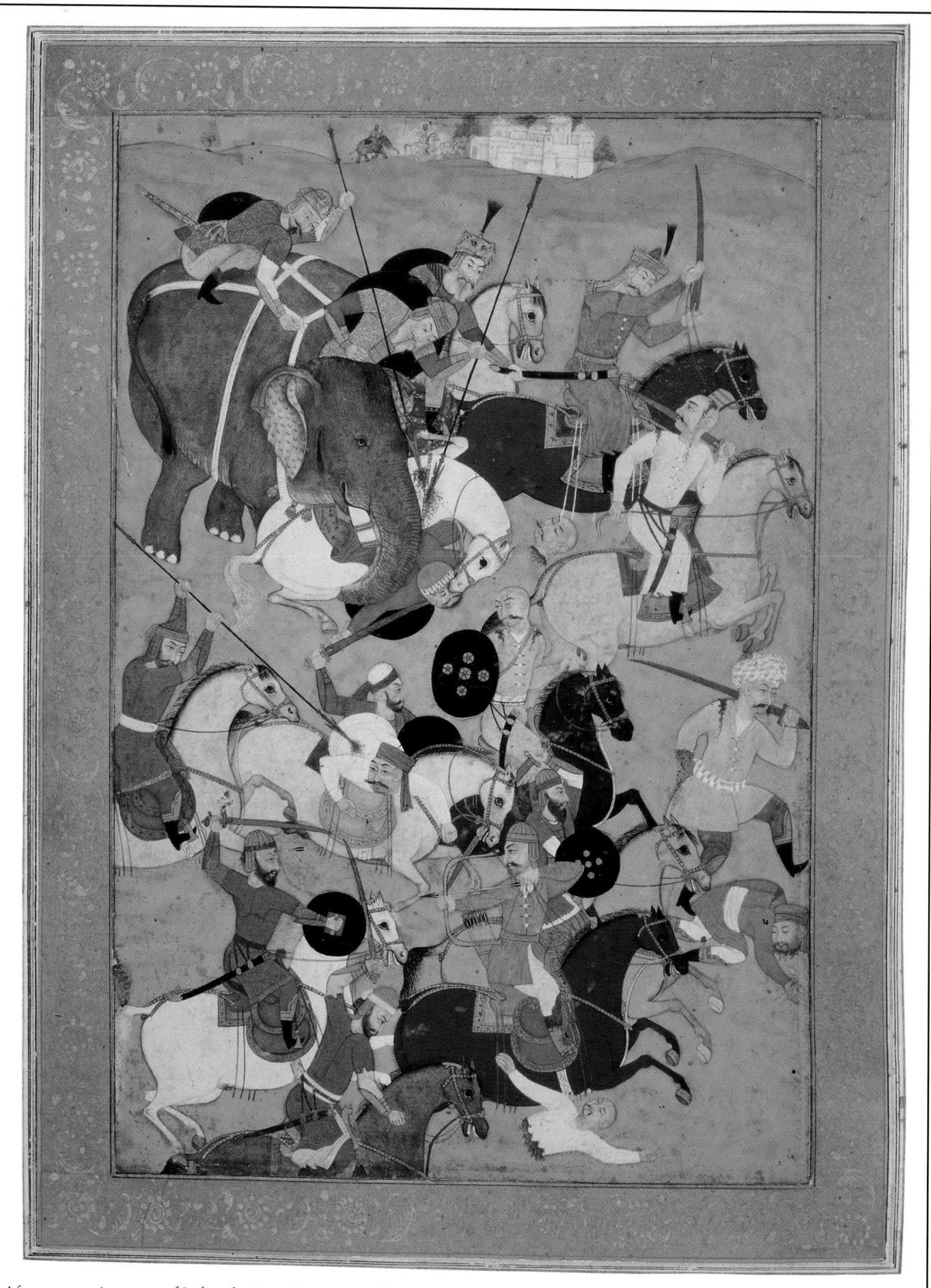

8   *After conquering most of India, the Mogul emperor Akbar tried to unite the many different peoples and religions.*

WORLD HISTORY

World History is an illustrated guide that highlights the most important topics and trends in world history and the people and the circumstances that helped to shape them. The eight sections each cover a distinct period in the story of humankind, from the earliest evidence of human activity to the complex world of the 1990s. A chronology of world events and a collection of brief biographies of notable men and women supplement the main text.

Areas as diverse as the arts, science and technology, religion, and the lives of people, both extraordinary and ordinary, are used to illuminate the major events of the past.

Together, the text and illustrations suggest some of the conclusions to be drawn from the study of history. Wars, it seems, rarely settle anything; rather they breed future conflict. History does not repeat itself; however, situations that are similar continually recur. Nor does *World History* assume that the history of the world is solely the story of Western nations. It shows that the achievements of the great civilizations of the Americas and Africa were substantial and that certain Asian civilizations have been more advanced than those of Europe.

Ken Hills

EARLY CIVILIZATIONS

Discovering the Past

History is not just the study of past events and famous people; it is also the story of human ideas and advancement. Until the 1800s, knowledge of history depended almost entirely on the study of written records. In the past two hundred years the science of archaeology has revealed much about the people who lived before writing was invented, about 5,000 years ago. Archaeologists can reconstruct the lives of prehistoric people by studying the objects, buildings, or bones that they left behind. Through these reconstructions we can learn about the first humans, who lived by hunting animals, as well as about those hunters who learned to plant their food and so became the first farmers. We can also find out about the lives of people who lived in the early civilizations of Europe, Africa, China, the Americas, India, and the Middle East.

RADIOCARBON DATING
The age of an ancient object can be fixed through radiocarbon dating. Living things absorb two kinds of carbon atoms—ordinary carbon, carbon 12; and radio carbon, carbon 14. When a plant or animal dies, the ratio of carbon 14 to carbon 12 decreases at a known rate. An archaeologist uses an instrument, a particle accelerator, to work out the age of an object by measuring its radiocarbon content.

▶ The earliest humanlike creatures so far discovered are australopithecines (southern apes). Their remains have been found in southern and eastern Africa, where they lived between 4 million and 1 million years ago.

▼ Archaeologists find out about the lives of people who lived before the first written records were made (prehistory) by studying their bones, their tools and utensils, and the remains of their buildings. A grid laid over the site is used to record exactly where each object was found.

Pottery

Stone knife

10

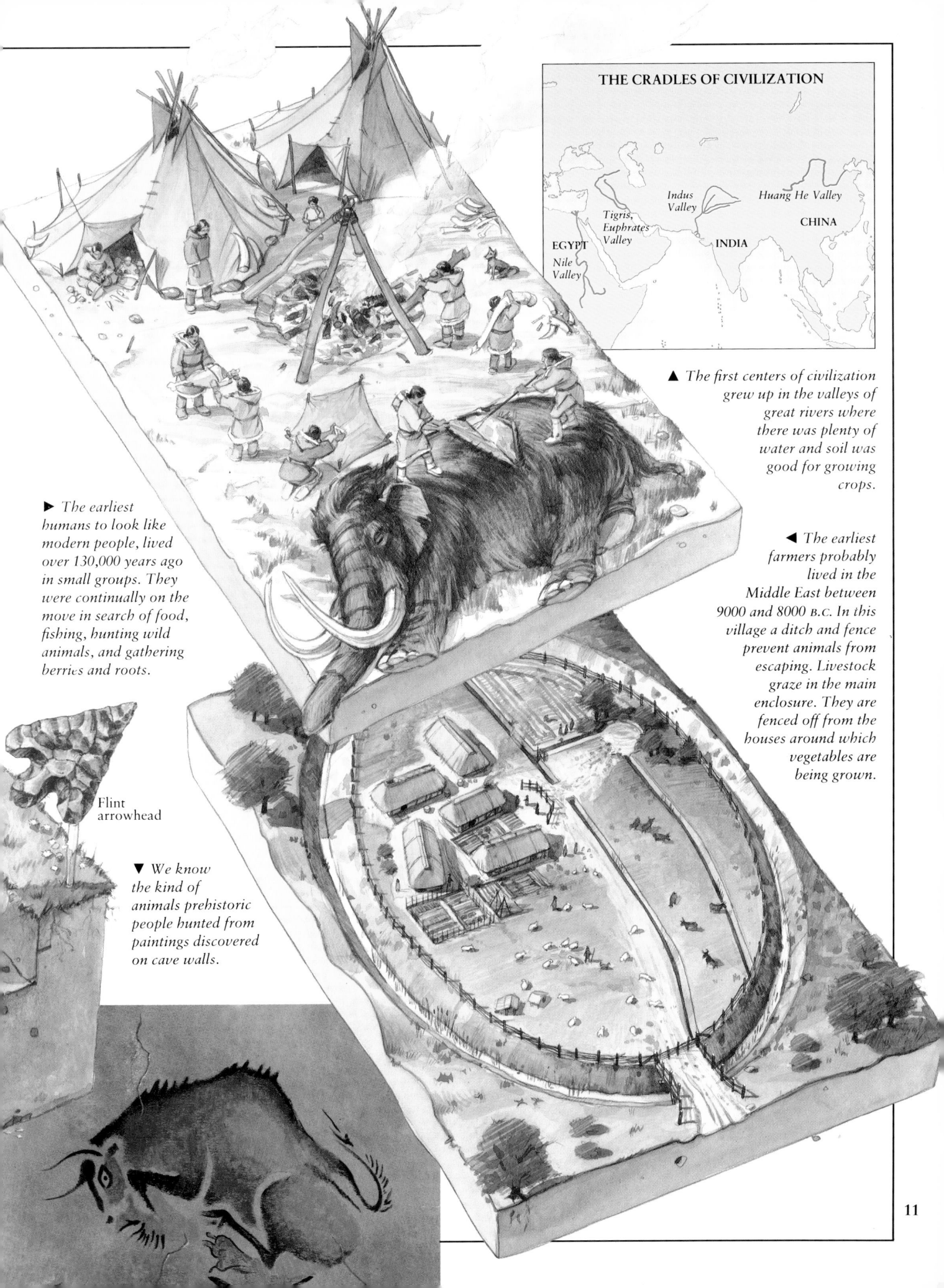

Indus
Valley

Huang He Valley

CHINA

Tigris,
Euphrates
Valley

EGYPT

INDIA

Nile
Valley

▲ The first centers of civilization grew up in the valleys of great rivers where there was plenty of water and soil was good for growing crops.

▶ The earliest humans to look like modern people, lived over 130,000 years ago in small groups. They were continually on the move in search of food, fishing, hunting wild animals, and gathering berries and roots.

◀ The earliest farmers probably lived in the Middle East between 9000 and 8000 B.C. In this village a ditch and fence prevent animals from escaping. Livestock graze in the main enclosure. They are fenced off from the houses around which vegetables are being grown.

Flint arrowhead

▼ We know the kind of animals prehistoric people hunted from paintings discovered on cave walls.

11

The Birth of Civilization

About five thousand years ago, in four separate areas of the world—the Nile valley, the Tiger-Euphrates valley, the Indus valley, and the Huang He valley—people in farming villages came together to establish towns. Later, they founded cities. The original farmers were compelled to work together in groups, to set up and manage the irrigation systems necessary to channel precious river water to the fields. This need for people to live together to control their environment may be the origin of civilization.

c.2371 B.C.–2316 B.C.
Reign of Sargon, first ruler of Sumeria

1550 B.C.–1070 B.C.
Ancient Egypt at height of its power

30 B.C.
Romans conquer Egypt

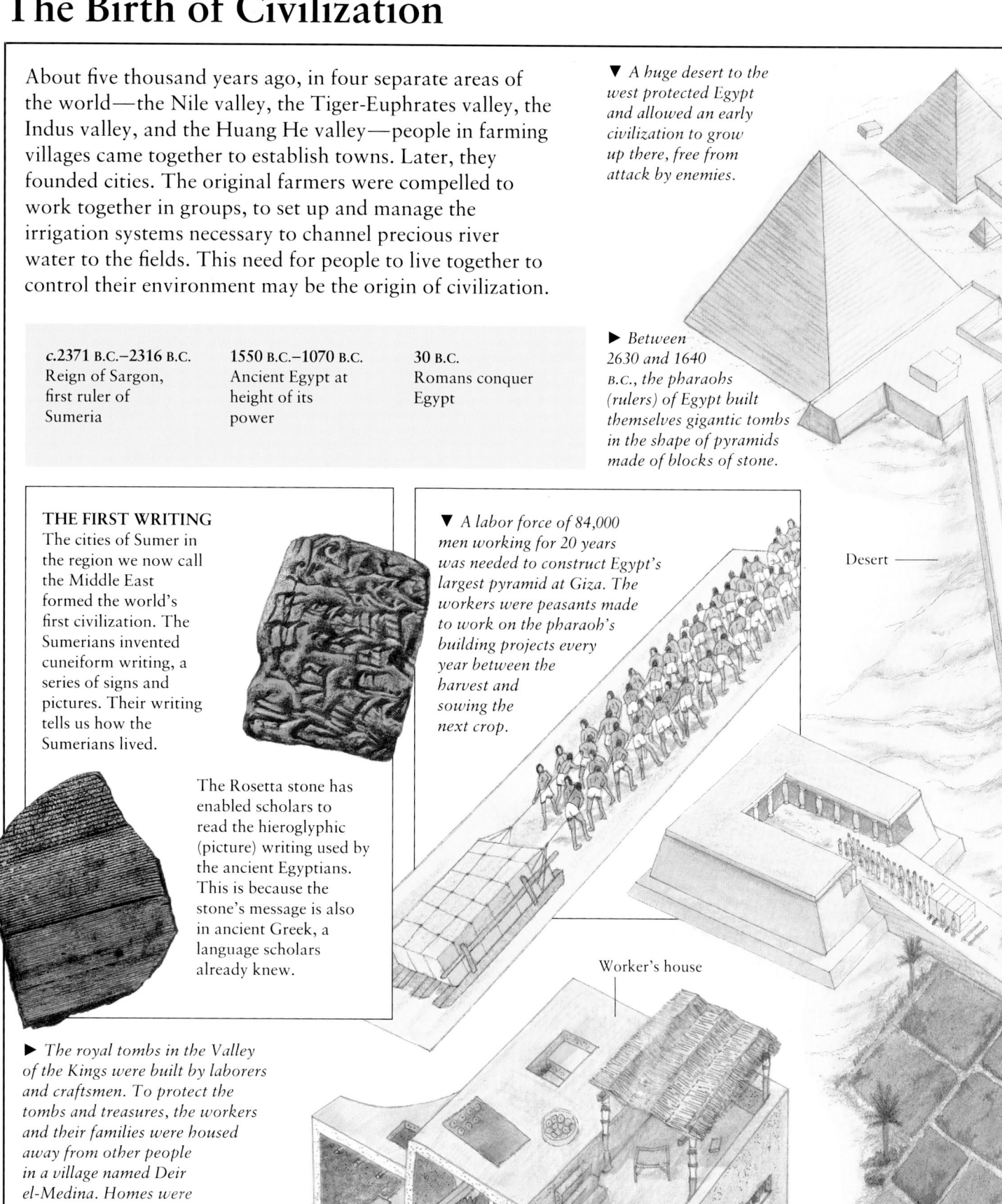

▼ *A huge desert to the west protected Egypt and allowed an early civilization to grow up there, free from attack by enemies.*

▶ *Between 2630 and 1640 B.C., the pharaohs (rulers) of Egypt built themselves gigantic tombs in the shape of pyramids made of blocks of stone.*

Desert ———

THE FIRST WRITING
The cities of Sumer in the region we now call the Middle East formed the world's first civilization. The Sumerians invented cuneiform writing, a series of signs and pictures. Their writing tells us how the Sumerians lived.

The Rosetta stone has enabled scholars to read the hieroglyphic (picture) writing used by the ancient Egyptians. This is because the stone's message is also in ancient Greek, a language scholars already knew.

▼ *A labor force of 84,000 men working for 20 years was needed to construct Egypt's largest pyramid at Giza. The workers were peasants made to work on the pharaoh's building projects every year between the harvest and sowing the next crop.*

Worker's house

▶ *The royal tombs in the Valley of the Kings were built by laborers and craftsmen. To protect the tombs and treasures, the workers and their families were housed away from other people in a village named Deir el-Medina. Homes were comfortable and had about four rooms. The village was surrounded by high walls and patrolled by guards day and night.*

12

EGYPTIAN SHIPS

Pictures and models found in tombs show what the ships of ancient Egypt looked like. The earliest boats were probably made of papyrus and used only for river sailing. A report from the time of King Snofru (*c*.2575 B.C.) tells of a fleet of 40 ships carrying a cargo of cedar. These vessels were made of wood and could be rowed or sailed and were heavier that the craft that sailed on the Nile. The Egyptians used them for trading with lands bordering the Mediterranean Sea.

Egyptian merchant ship, *c*.1500 B.C.

▼ *For nearly 4,000 years from 4000 B.C., the eastern Mediterranean was dominated by a succession of conquering nations: Babylonians, Assyrians, and Persians. The most warlike were the Assyrians, whose fierce and ruthless soldiers made the Assyrian army the most effective the ancient world had yet seen.*

Covered raised road

Irrigated fields

Persian foot soldier

◀ *Every summer, the Nile overflowed onto the surrounding land. As Egypt had hardly any rain, farmers dug canals from the river to bring water to their fields after the floods had gone down. The arrival of floods made sure that the crops grew and fed the Egyptian people.*

Babylonian archer

—Nile River

— Temple

Assyrian war chariot and archer

FURTHER FACTS

● There are over 500 signs in cuneiform writing. It was taught in schools called "tablet houses" after the clay tablets on which the signs were written.
● In ancient Egypt five holy days celebrated the chief gods; these were all rest days.

The Beginnings of Beliefs

Every human society has had some form of religion. That the earliest peoples believed in life after death is proved by the way corpses were buried with tools or pots for use in the afterlife. As the great civilizations developed in Asia, the Middle East, India, and China, religious practices became more elaborate. Priests were appointed to make sure that religious ceremonies were properly observed. From 1500 B.C. to 500 B.C. many of the great religions of the world began to take shape within these civilizations.

c.1500-600 B.C.
Hindu religion develops in India

c.1200 B.C.s
Beginning of Jewish religion, which worships one god, Yahweh

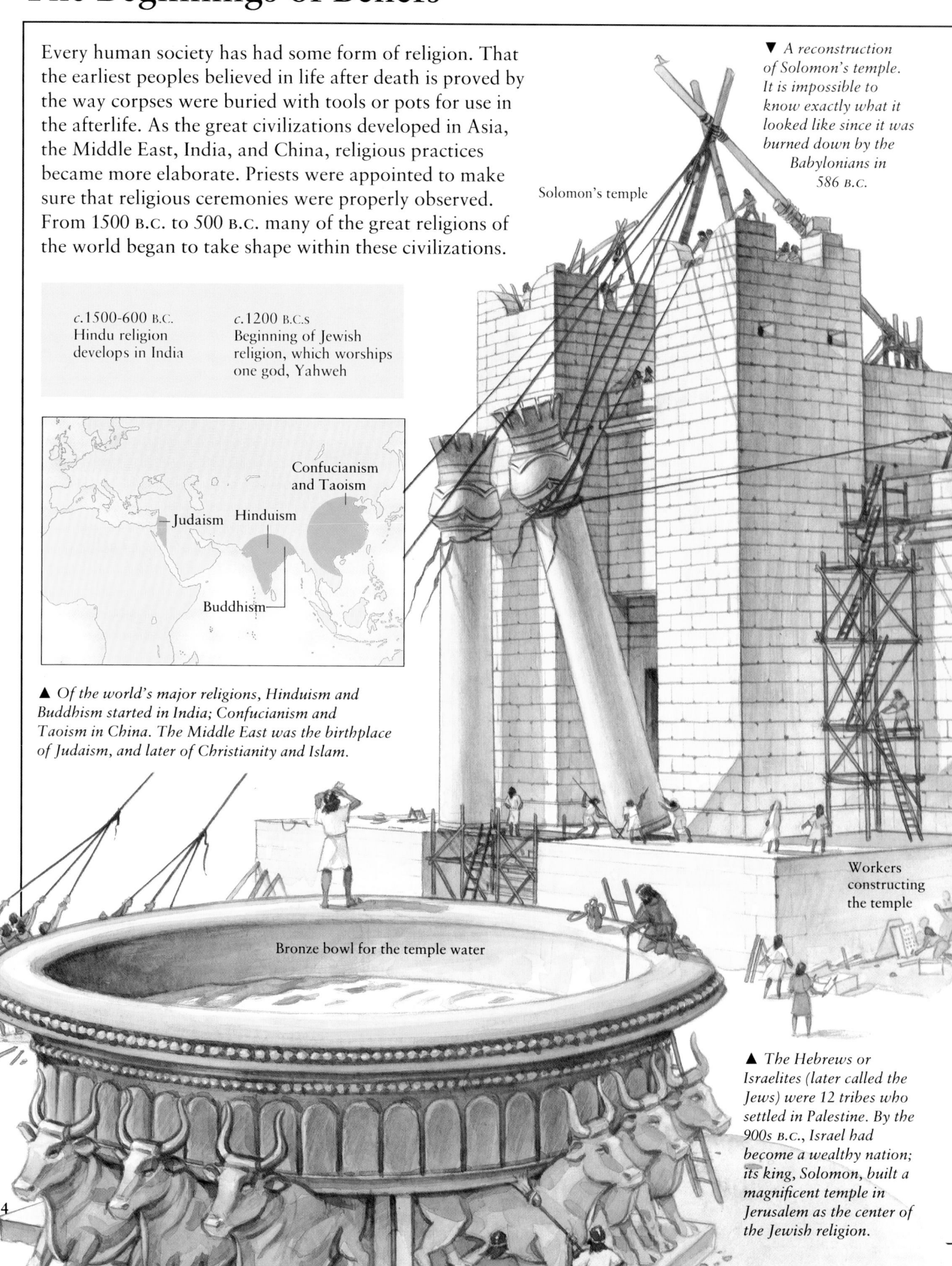

▲ Of the world's major religions, Hinduism and Buddhism started in India; Confucianism and Taoism in China. The Middle East was the birthplace of Judaism, and later of Christianity and Islam.

Solomon's temple

▼ A reconstruction of Solomon's temple. It is impossible to know exactly what it looked like since it was burned down by the Babylonians in 586 B.C.

Workers constructing the temple

Bronze bowl for the temple water

▲ The Hebrews or Israelites (later called the Jews) were 12 tribes who settled in Palestine. By the 900s B.C., Israel had become a wealthy nation; its king, Solomon, built a magnificent temple in Jerusalem as the center of the Jewish religion.

14

EASTERN RELIGIONS

Of the two great Indian religions only Hinduism has no founder. It combines the beliefs of the Aryan tribes who invaded India in about 1500 B.C. with the religion of the people they conquered. Buddhism, India's other great religion, was founded in the 6th century B.C. Three centuries later, Emperor Asoka was converted to Buddhism. By the end of his reign, Buddhism had spread throughout India and beyond into Sri Lanka. The two ancient religions of China are Taoism and Confucianism. The story of the founding of Judaism is told in the book known to Jews as the Hebrew Bible and to Christians as the Old Testament.

Siva

▶ *Hinduism is the term used for the religious beliefs and practices of India. Among its most important gods is Siva, who is believed to be both creator and destroyer.*

▶ *Gautama, the Buddha, lived c.563–480 B.C.. He was a wealthy prince who gave up his life of luxury to become a poor wandering preacher in northern India.*

The Buddha

Lao-Tzu

◀ *Taoism came from ancient Chinese folk religions in about 500 B.C. This statue is of a Taoist founder, Lao-Tzu, riding on a green ox.*

▶ *Confucius (c.551– c.479 B.C.) was a great Chinese philosopher or thinker. He was not a spiritual leader, but he taught the practical advantages of kindness, respect, and personal effort.*

Confucius

FURTHER FACTS

● The followers of early religions worshiped many gods. The Jews were the first people to believe in one god, whom they called Yahweh.
● Taoism has more gods than most other religions; some of these gods are famous people, others are ancestors.
● Another major ancient religion is Shinto, the native religion of Japan; Shinto developed from early folk beliefs.

15

The Greeks

Ancient Greece was not one state with its own government. It was made up of many independent communities called "city-states," who all shared the same language and culture. Between 800 B.C. and 400 B.C. the people of these miniature countries, particularly those of the most successful city, Athens, established many of the ideas that underlie Western civilization. But although democratic government started in Greece, only men could become citizens and vote—women (and slaves) were excluded.

THE MINOANS
The Minoans were traders who, between 2000 and 1100 B.C., established the first major civilization in Europe on the island of Crete. *(Above)* A decorated Minoan vase and a frieze depicting a religious or magical rite that involved leaping over bulls.

c.2000–1100 B.C.	c.800–338 B.C.	323 B.C.
Minoan civilization	Golden age of Greek civilization	Alexander's death ends great age of Greece

▶ *About 1000 B.C. many of the original Greek cities had become overcrowded. By 500 B.C., groups of citizens had left the mainland and settled in other parts of the Mediterranean.*

◀ *Well-armed Greek hoplites (foot-soldiers) were almost unbeatable on land. At sea, powerful Greek triremes rowed by 150 oarsmen overcame all opposition.*

ANCIENT GREECE AND ITS COLONIES c.500 B.C.

Trapezus
Sinope
GAUL
Byzantium
MACEDONIA
ITALY
ASIA MINOR
CORSICA
Rome
GREECE
Delphi · Athens
SICILY
Olympia · Sparta
CYPRUS
Sidon
Tyre
RHODES
SARDINIA
Syracuse
CRETE
Carthage
Cyrene
Alexandria
EGYPT

ALEXANDER THE GREAT
Alexander, king of Macedon, was one of the greatest generals of all time. He died in 323 B.C., aged only 32, leaving behind an empire that extended from Greece to India. In 333 B.C. at Issus *(below)*, Alexander won a great victory when his troops defeated a much larger Persian army led by the Persian king Darius *(right)*. By 330 B.C. Alexander had conquered all of the Persian empire.

EMPIRE OF ALEXANDER THE GREAT c.500 B.C.

MACEDONIA
· Athens
CYPRUS · Issus
MESOPOTAMIA
PERSIA
Mediterranean Sea
AFGHANISTAN
· Alexandria
Babylon
EGYPT

◀ The Greeks did not invent their alphabet. They adopted a set of signs used in Syria and modified them to form a simple alphabet of 24 letters.

▶ Greek plays were acted in open-air theaters. Some theaters seated over 10,000 people. Men wearing masks played all the parts.

▲ A bronze statue of a Spartan girl athlete. The city of Sparta was a powerful rival of Athens. Spartan women lived the freest lives of any women in ancient Greece.

▶ An "acropolis" was a fortress on a hill where citizens took shelter in times of danger. The Acropolis in Athens is famous for its shrines and temples, such as the Parthenon.

▶ In Athens, all citizens over 30 served on juries. Each juror was given two bronze tokens. Tokens with a solid center meant "innocent." Those with a hole meant "guilty."

▶ The Greeks told stories of their gods in which they behaved like ordinary people. On this decorated plate Hades, god of the underworld, drinks with his wife, the goddess Persephone.

17

The Rise of Rome

According to tradition, Rome was founded by Romulus and Remus in 753 B.C. Until about 500 B.C., Rome was one of several towns ruled by the kings of Etruria in the region now called Italy. After the Etruscans were overthrown, the city of Rome became a republic. The Romans were a warlike people who sought to gain new territory. Their greatest rivals in southern Europe were the Carthaginians, whom they defeated in the three Punic Wars. By 44 B.C. the Romans controlled most of the Mediterranean lands.

*c.*500 B.C.
Founding of
Roman republic

264 B.C.-146 B.C.
Three Punic Wars
against Carthage

27 B.C.
Roman republic
ends; empire begins
under Augustus

▼ *In amphitheaters the Romans watched wild animals or gladiators fighting each other to the death.*

▲ *Legend says that Rome's founders, Romulus and Remus, were abandoned as babies but were found by a she-wolf who fed them on her milk.*

THE ROMAN CIRCUS

Rome's chariot-racing stadium, the Circus Maximus, was 1,800 ft (550 m) by 600 ft (180 m). The stands could hold up to 250,000 spectators, more than a quarter of the city's population.

▼ *Most Roman shops were small. Jewelers, bakers, carpenters, shoemakers, tanners, and hardware dealers made what they sold in workshops attached to their premises. In this smithy (left), the blacksmith's tools are shown separately. Everyday objects such as keys, household lamps, and coins (below) were all handmade.*

▼ *The Romans were greatly influenced by Greek drama and both plays and theaters were copied from the Greeks. In this mosaic from a house in Pompeii, Roman actors and musicians are preparing to perform in a Greek play.*

Key

Oil lamp

Coins

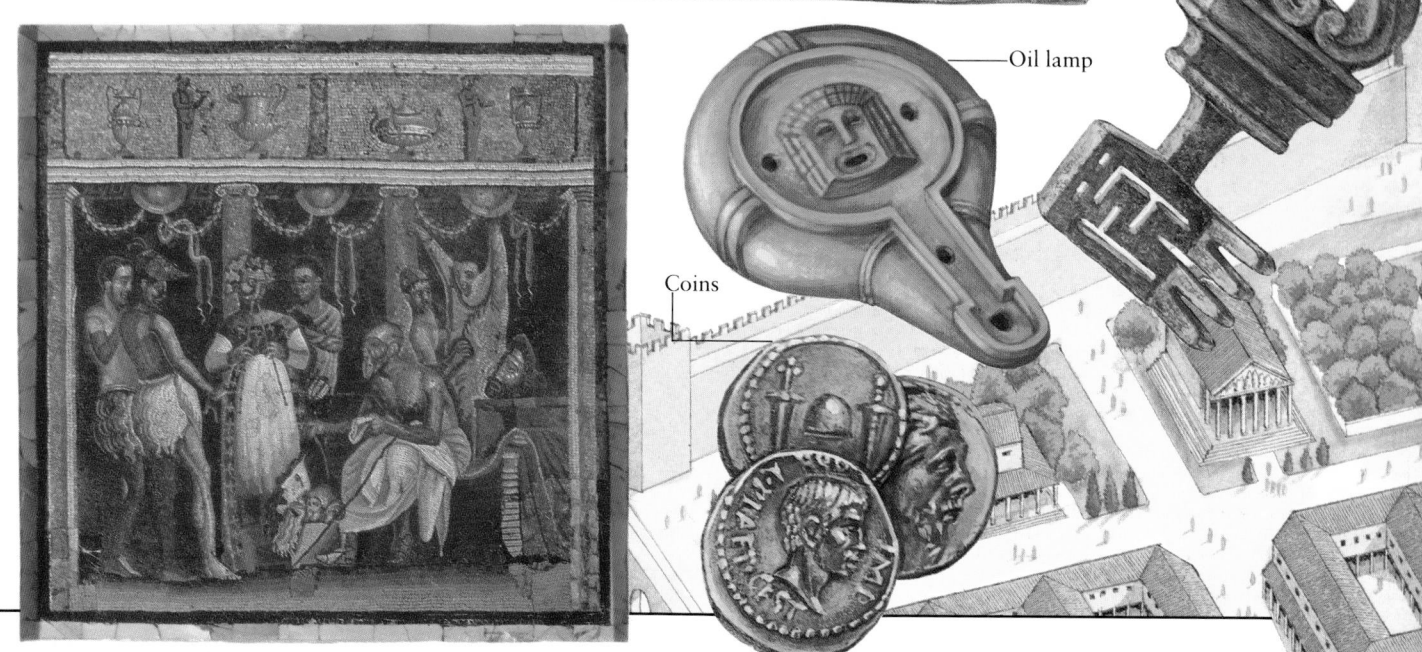

GLADIATORS
Gladiators were slaves or criminals who were trained in special schools to fight each other or wild animals in the amphitheaters.

POMPEII
In A.D. 79 the volcano Vesuvius erupted, burying the Roman port and resort town of Pompeii in southern Italy. In 1748 the town was rediscovered. Volcanic ash and cinders had preserved the ruins and the shapes of the bodies of citizens, who were unable to get away in time. A baker *(above)* was found beside the loaf of bread he had just baked.

HORSE RACES
Vast crowds flocked to watch and bet on chariot races. Charioteers raced in teams wearing team colors. Some fans formed clubs.

◄ *The Romans built superb roads throughout their empire. The roads were brilliantly engineered across marshes, tunneled under hills, and carved along the sides of mountains.*

► *Baths were not merely places to wash in but were centers where people went to relax and meet friends. Fresh water was brought from the hills to the towns by aqueducts and pipes.*

▼ *Grand houses were owned by rich citizens. In the country, they lived with their servants in villas on big estates.*

► *The Romans worshiped a number of gods and each of their many temples was dedicated to a particular god or goddess.*

▲ *The forum was originally the town marketplace. Later it became an open area surrounded by buildings where business was carried out.*

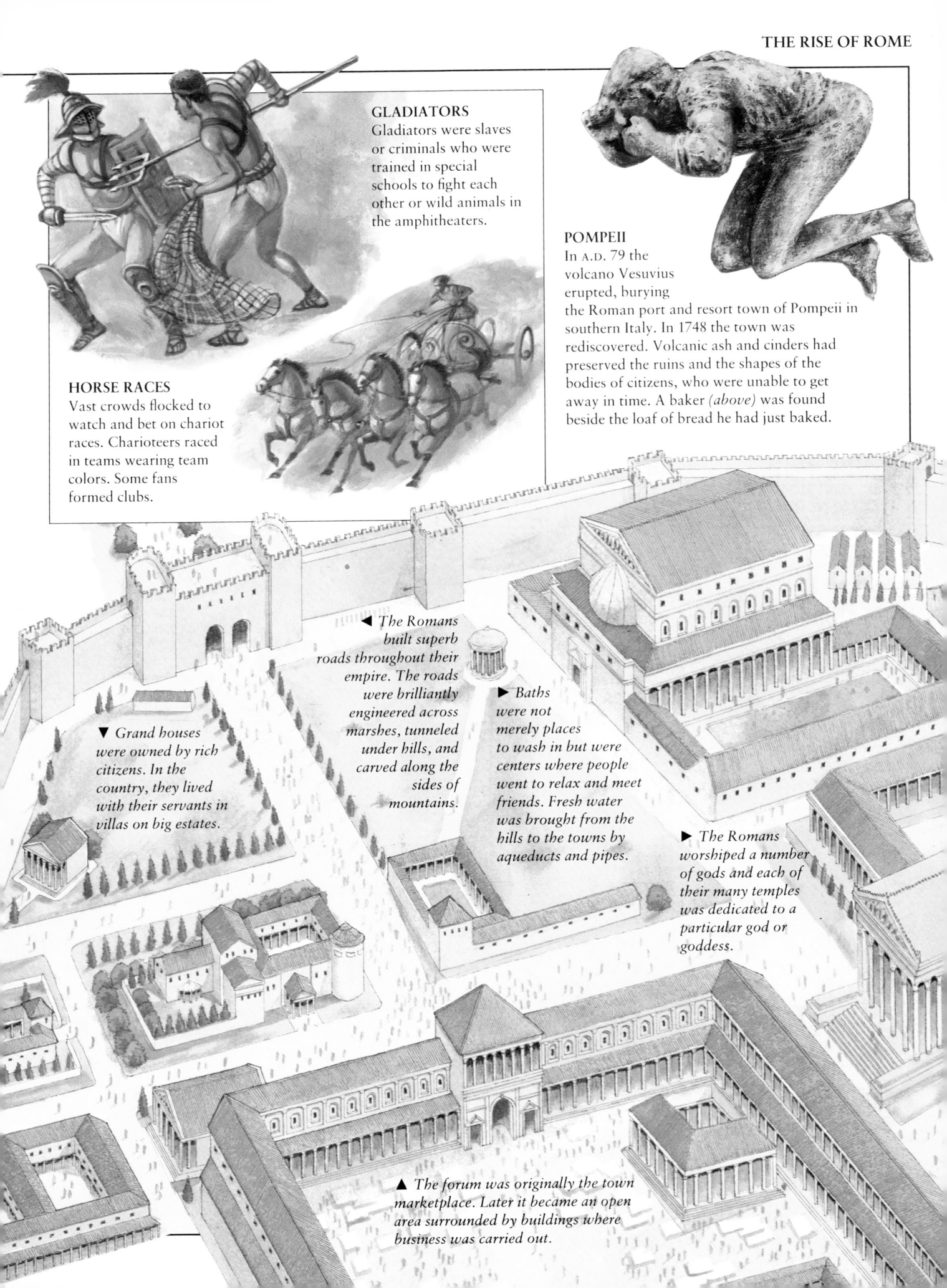

The Roman Empire

The empire founded by emperor Augustus in 27 B.C. lasted for nearly 500 years. At its greatest territorial extent, about A.D. 100, it stretched from Spain in the west to the Persian Gulf in the east. For two hundred years, the Roman empire was relatively peaceful. But the 3rd century A.D. saw the beginnings of turmoil as migrating tribes attacked the empire's eastern frontiers. Eventually, the empire was split into an Eastern empire with its capital in Constantinople, and a Western empire ruled from Rome.

27 B.C.–A.D. 14	A.D. 395	A.D. 476
Reign of Augustus, first Roman emperor	Roman empire split in two by Theodosius	Romulus Augustus, last emperor of Western empire deposed

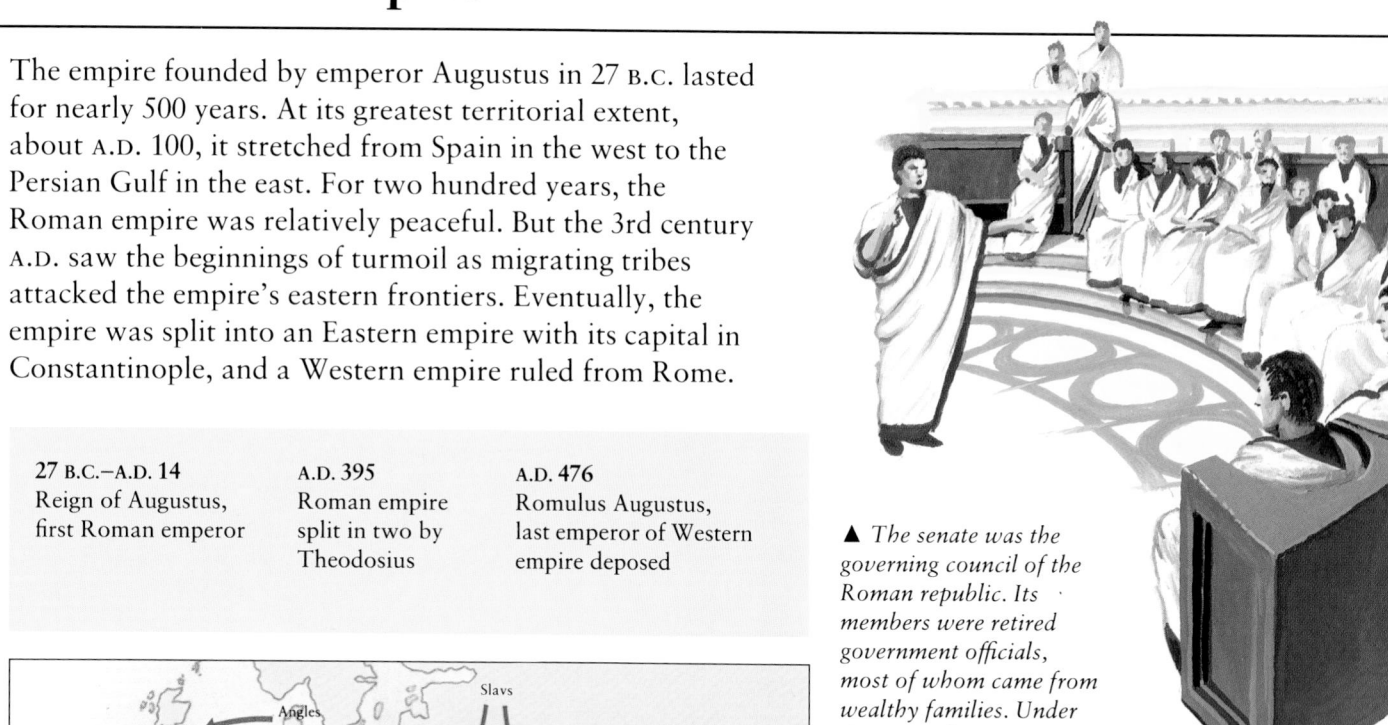

▲ The senate was the governing council of the Roman republic. Its members were retired government officials, most of whom came from wealthy families. Under Augustus the senate gradually lost its power.

▼ A legion was an infantry unit of the Roman army. It was made up of ordinary soldiers called legionaries commanded by officers (centurians). Standard-bearers carried the legion's emblem. The legions' victories built the Roman empire.

Centurion

Legionary

Standard bearer

ROME'S ACHIEVEMENTS
Between about 27 B.C. and A.D. 200 the Roman empire was prosperous and peaceful. Travel was relatively quick and safe along the network of excellent roads which linked all parts of the empire.

A common coinage, language, and legal system encouraged trade. Towns had fine public buildings and clean water. Outside the towns, irrigation and better tools led to more efficient farming methods.

▲ The Roman empire was constantly under attack from invading tribes seeking land and plunder. Rome was finally overrun by Alaric, leader of the Visigoths, in A.D. 410.

▶ Roman legions were equipped with machines for attacking enemy strongholds. Catapults shot large arrows. The ballista was similar but fired stones.

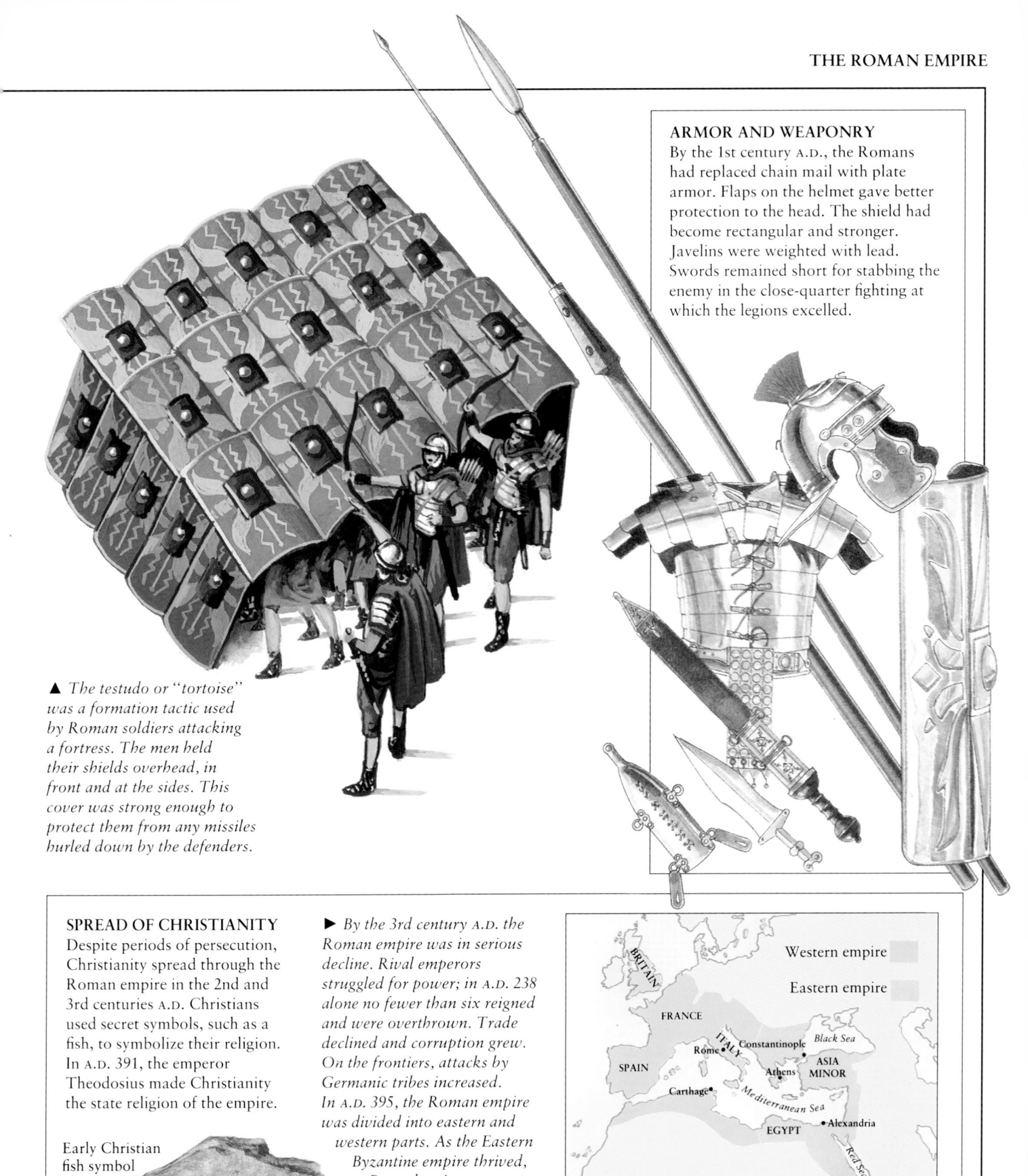

ARMOR AND WEAPONRY
By the 1st century A.D., the Romans had replaced chain mail with plate armor. Flaps on the helmet gave better protection to the head. The shield had become rectangular and stronger. Javelins were weighted with lead. Swords remained short for stabbing the enemy in the close-quarter fighting at which the legions excelled.

▲ The testudo or "tortoise" was a formation tactic used by Roman soldiers attacking a fortress. The men held their shields overhead, in front and at the sides. This cover was strong enough to protect them from any missiles hurled down by the defenders.

SPREAD OF CHRISTIANITY
Despite periods of persecution, Christianity spread through the Roman empire in the 2nd and 3rd centuries A.D. Christians used secret symbols, such as a fish, to symbolize their religion. In A.D. 391, the emperor Theodosius made Christianity the state religion of the empire.

Early Christian fish symbol

▶ By the 3rd century A.D. the Roman empire was in serious decline. Rival emperors struggled for power; in A.D. 238 alone no fewer than six reigned and were overthrown. Trade declined and corruption grew. On the frontiers, attacks by Germanic tribes increased. In A.D. 395, the Roman empire was divided into eastern and western parts. As the Eastern Byzantine empire thrived, Rome lost its power until it eventually disintegrated. The Western empire ended when a Germanic tribe deposed the last emperor.

Western empire
Eastern empire

BRITAIN
FRANCE
SPAIN
ITALY
Rome
Constantinople
Black Sea
ASIA MINOR
Athens
Carthage
Mediterranean Sea
EGYPT
Alexandria
Red Sea

▶ The Emperor Constantine was converted to Christianity by a vision of a flaming cross. In A.D. 313 he issued an order allowing Christians to worship.

THE MIDDLE AGES

Raiders and Invaders

The Middle Ages is the time in European history between ancient and modern times. The period is also known as the medieval period, from the Latin words *medium* (middle) and *aevum* (age). Early in the Middle Ages, western European civilization went through a period of upheaval and chaos as a succession of Germanic tribes surged through the former Roman empire. Meanwhile, the rise of Islam in the Near East gave birth to a dynamic and warlike culture which gradually spread into southern and northern Europe. Elsewhere, powerful empires and highly-developed civilizations prospered in Asia and the Americas. By the late Middle Ages, the increased power of the European kings and the civilizing force of the Christian Church helped Europe recover from centuries of invasion, lawlessness, and economic breakdown.

1066	1218–1224
William of Normandy conquers England	Genghis Khan's Mongols reach southeast Europe

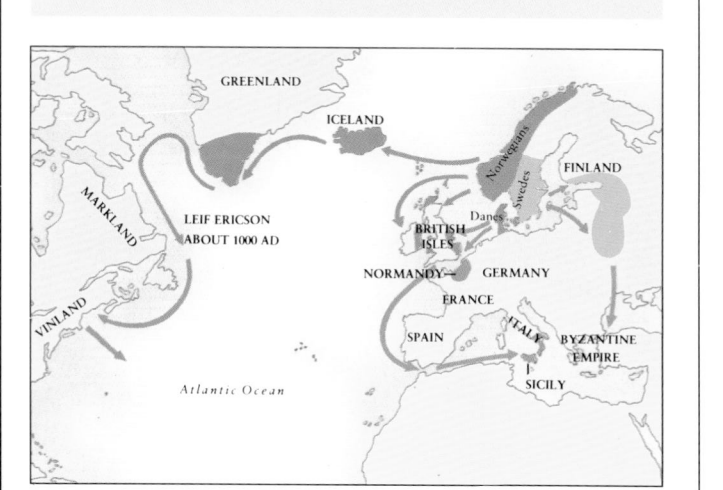

▲ The Vikings were traders and warriors from Scandinavia who raided, and later settled, in parts of northern Europe between the 9th and 11th centuries.

Thor

Odin

◄ The Vikings believed in many gods, the most important of whom was Odin. Odin's son Thor was the god of thunder and war. Thursday (Thor's day) is named after him.

VIKING BOATS
Viking longships, or war ships, were low and narrow. They were designed for both sailing and rowing and were shallow enough to be rowed up rivers. The sides were lined with the rowers' painted shields. Viking cargo ships were higher and wider. The largest could carry up to 38 tons of cargo.

◄ *In the 1100s, tribes of nomadic peoples called Mongols, living in central Asia, united under a great warrior, Genghis Khan. The Mongols were to conquer a vast empire that stretched over China, and India, the Near East, and into parts of Europe.*

THE DOMESDAY BOOK

In 1085, William the Conqueror decided to find out who owned land and property and how much tax they should pay on it. His officials toured England recording the names of landowners, their holdings, and how much their possessions were worth. The record of the survey was called the Domesday Book.

► *There are many romantic stories about the British king, Arthur, his court at Camelot, and the knights of the Round Table. There may be some truth in the legends. One early chronicle tells of a leader named Arthur who led the British against Saxon invaders in the 800s.*

Arthur and the knights of the Round Table

THE NORMAN CONQUEST

The Normans were descended from Vikings who had settled in northern France. In 1066, their leader, Duke William, invaded England to seize the throne from King Harold. The English were routed at the battle of Hastings and William became king.

▼ *The Bayeux Tapestry is a gigantic picture story recording the Norman conquest of England. It was woven on the orders of Bishop Odo, half brother of William the Conqueror. The section shown depicts Harold's death in the battle of Hastings.*

After his successful invasion, William the Conqueror consolidated his rule by crushing any revolts by English rebels

Christianity and Islam

Christianity originated in Palestine, Islam arose in Arabia; both regions of the Middle East. Christianity grew out of Judaism, the religion of the Jews, in the 1st century A.D. Six centuries later, the prophet Muhammad preached to the Arab people that a single god, Allah, should replace the many gods they had worshiped before. Both faiths spread rapidly. Christianity became the dominant religion of Europe, but was in peril of being overwhelmed by Arab armies until an Arab invasion was halted in France in 732.

▼ During the early Middle Ages some Christians who believed they were called to devote their lives to God, set up a number of small private communities. They did not mix with the rest of society. Women entered convents as nuns. Men became monks and lived in monasteries.

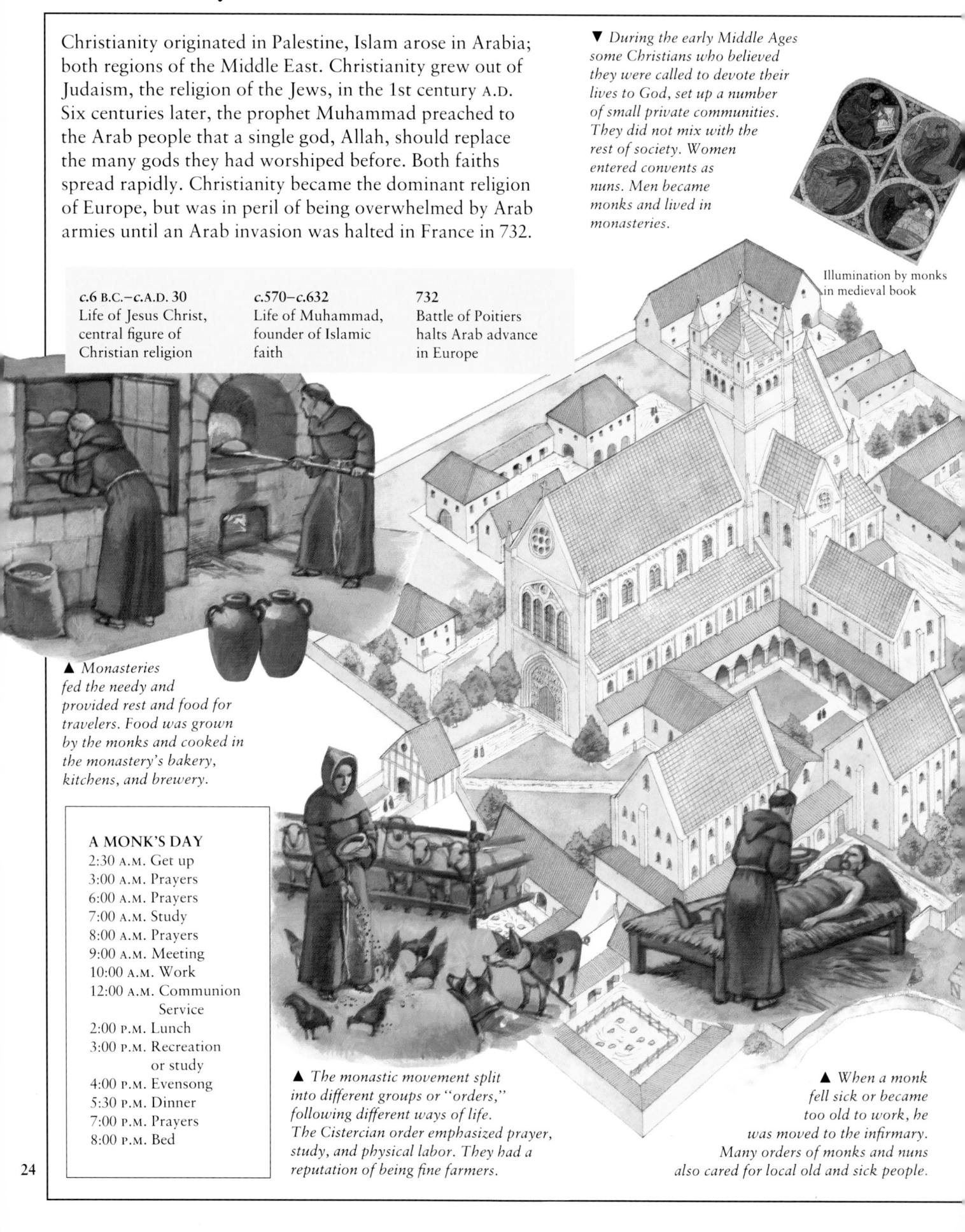

Illumination by monks in medieval book

c.6 B.C.–c.A.D. 30	c.570–c.632	732
Life of Jesus Christ, central figure of Christian religion	Life of Muhammad, founder of Islamic faith	Battle of Poitiers halts Arab advance in Europe

▲ Monasteries fed the needy and provided rest and food for travelers. Food was grown by the monks and cooked in the monastery's bakery, kitchens, and brewery.

A MONK'S DAY
2:30 A.M. Get up
3:00 A.M. Prayers
6:00 A.M. Prayers
7:00 A.M. Study
8:00 A.M. Prayers
9:00 A.M. Meeting
10:00 A.M. Work
12:00 A.M. Communion Service
2:00 P.M. Lunch
3:00 P.M. Recreation or study
4:00 P.M. Evensong
5:30 P.M. Dinner
7:00 P.M. Prayers
8:00 P.M. Bed

▲ The monastic movement split into different groups or "orders," following different ways of life. The Cistercian order emphasized prayer, study, and physical labor. They had a reputation of being fine farmers.

▲ When a monk fell sick or became too old to work, he was moved to the infirmary. Many orders of monks and nuns also cared for local old and sick people.

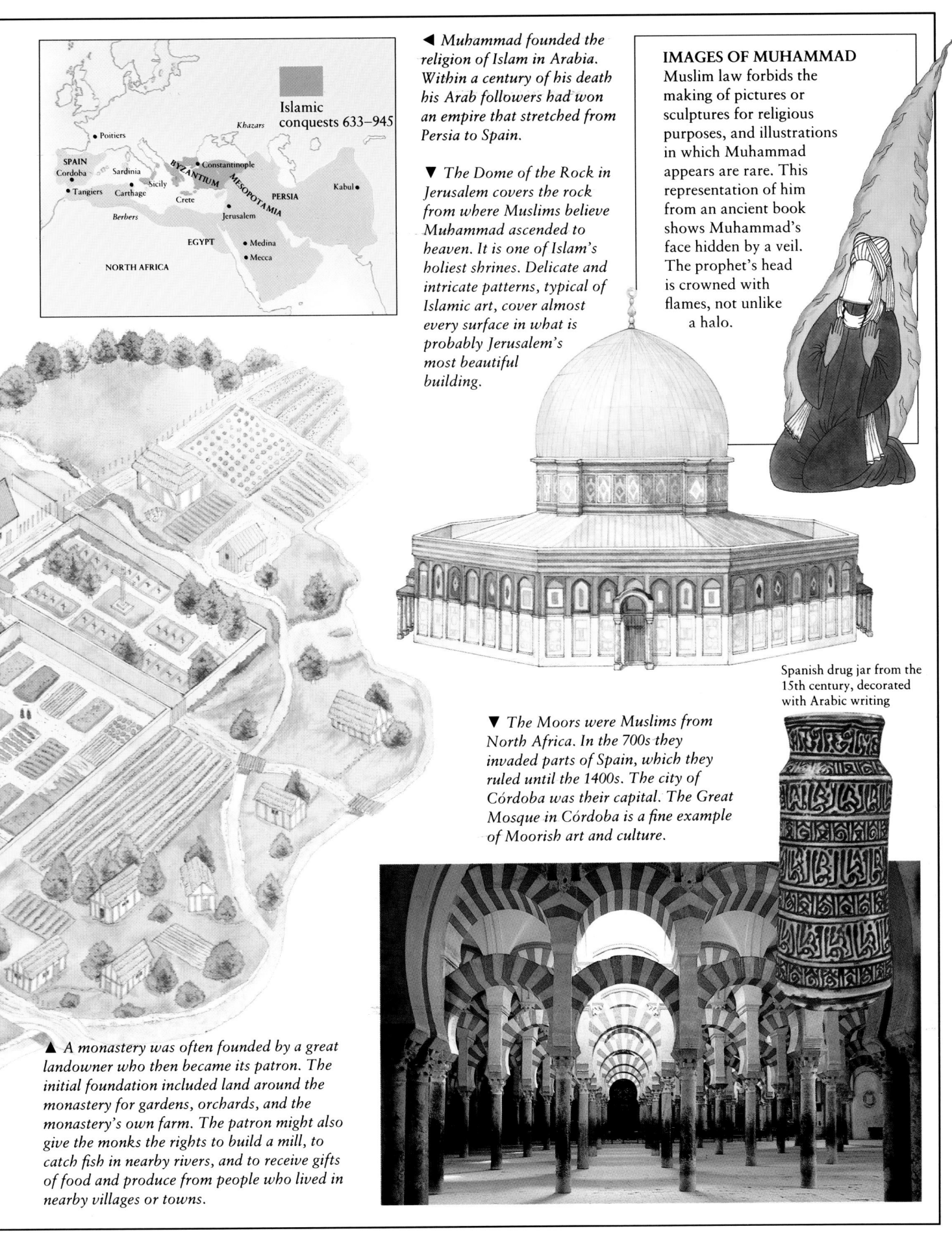

Islamic conquests 633–945

◄ *Muhammad founded the religion of Islam in Arabia. Within a century of his death his Arab followers had won an empire that stretched from Persia to Spain.*

▼ *The Dome of the Rock in Jerusalem covers the rock from where Muslims believe Muhammad ascended to heaven. It is one of Islam's holiest shrines. Delicate and intricate patterns, typical of Islamic art, cover almost every surface in what is probably Jerusalem's most beautiful building.*

IMAGES OF MUHAMMAD
Muslim law forbids the making of pictures or sculptures for religious purposes, and illustrations in which Muhammad appears are rare. This representation of him from an ancient book shows Muhammad's face hidden by a veil. The prophet's head is crowned with flames, not unlike a halo.

Spanish drug jar from the 15th century, decorated with Arabic writing

▼ *The Moors were Muslims from North Africa. In the 700s they invaded parts of Spain, which they ruled until the 1400s. The city of Córdoba was their capital. The Great Mosque in Córdoba is a fine example of Moorish art and culture.*

▲ *A monastery was often founded by a great landowner who then became its patron. The initial foundation included land around the monastery for gardens, orchards, and the monastery's own farm. The patron might also give the monks the rights to build a mill, to catch fish in nearby rivers, and to receive gifts of food and produce from people who lived in nearby villages or towns.*

The Crusades

During the Middle Ages, many Christian pilgrims from Europe traveled to Palestine to worship at places associated with the life of Jesus Christ. In 1071, a Muslim people, the Seljuk Turks, conquered Palestine and brought these pilgrimages to an end. When Pope Urban II summoned European Christians to take up arms against the Muslims, thousands of knights and ordinary soldiers answered his call. For two centuries Christian armies strove to regain Palestine in wars called the Crusades.

1095–1099
First Crusade captures Jerusalem. Four Christian kingdoms set up in Holy Land

1187
Saladin, Sultan of Egypt, recaptures Jerusalem

1217–1221
The Fifth and last major Crusade

▼ *During the Crusades Muslims were called "Saracens" by the Christians. The Saracens were expert warriors on horseback.*

▼ *During the Third Crusade Richard I of England won a major victory when his troops captured the Saracen fortress of Acre and defeated the army of the Muslim leader Saladin at Arsuf. This victory earned Richard the name of "Lion-Heart." Fighting in the Holy Lands or France, Richard seldom visited England. He is buried next to his mother, Queen Eleanor, at Fontrevault in France.*

▶ *Among the most feared Christian warriors were the Knights Templars. They were members of a religious military order who chose to serve God by fighting rather than through prayer.*

▲ *The Crusaders built castles to defend the lands they conquered. The largest and strongest Crusader castle was Krak des Chevaliers. It was built by the Knights Hospitalers (a military religious order) and lies in the desert of what is now Syria on a hilltop 2,460 ft. (750 m) high.*

During the Crusades it was garrisoned by up to 2,000 men. It held out against many attacks but finally fell to the Saracens in 1271 when the defenders were starved into surrender after a year's siege.

Crusader castle of Krak des Chevaliers

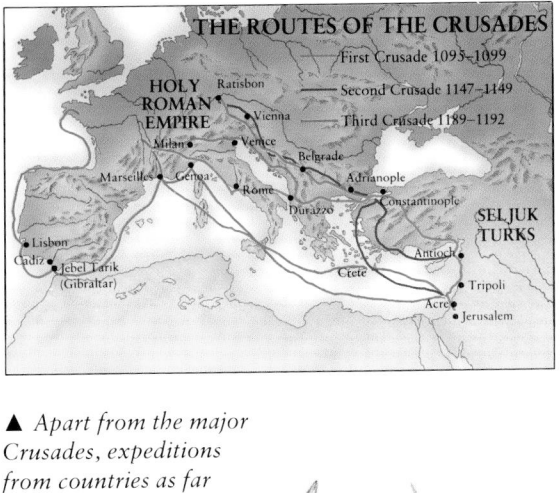

THE ROUTES OF THE CRUSADES

First Crusade 1095–1099
Second Crusade 1147–1149
Third Crusade 1189–1192

HOLY ROMAN EMPIRE

Ratisbon
Vienna
Milan
Venice
Belgrade
Marseilles
Genoa
Rome
Durazzo
Adrianople
Constantinople
Crete
Antioch
Lisbon
Cadiz
Jebel Tarik (Gibraltar)
Tripoli
Acre
Jerusalem

SELJUK TURKS

◄ *Pilgrimages are journeys to holy places. The men and women who went on pilgrimages to the Holy Land often brought back a palm tree branch to lay on the altar of their church at home.*

FURTHER FACTS

The capture of Jerusalem made the First Crusade (1095–1099) the most successful Crusade for the Christians. In 1187, Muslim armies took Jerusalem. and the Christians never recaptured it. The last Christian stronghold at Acre in Palestine fell to the Muslims in 1291.

▲ *Apart from the major Crusades, expeditions from countries as far away as Norway went to fight in the Holy Land.*

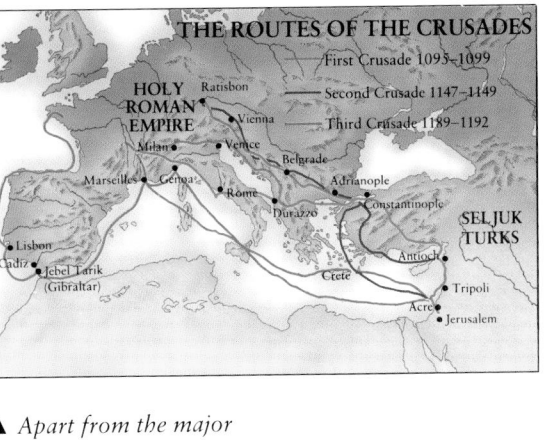

◄ *In 1212, thousands of children from France and Germany joined a Crusade. They were inspired by a French boy, Stephen, and a German boy, Nicholas. Neither group reached the Holy Land. Many died of hunger or disease. Some were sold as slaves.*

CHIVALRY, HERALDRY, AND TOURNAMENTS

The ideal knight was brave in battle, loyal to his lord, and protected women. These rules of behavior were known as "chivalry." Fully-armed knights displayed a sign on their shields or on their surcoat in order to be recognized in battle. During the 1100s each design or "coat of arms" became the property of a particular family, a system known as "heraldry." Knights fought mock battles called "jousts" in tournaments (*right*). They used blunted weapons and wore special armor. Each joust started with two knights charging each other with lances.

Jousting armor

War and Plague

The 1300s and 1400s were a disastrous period for Europe. The Hundred Years' War, fought when England tried to gain lands in France, was a calamity with parts of France laid waste by armies. In the mid-1300s, rich and poor alike died in the plague, known as the Black Death. Many peasants survived only to die of starvation as crops remained unpicked. About 25 million people may have died. Disorder became widespread. In France, Italy, and England peasant revolts were crushed by the authorities.

1337–1453
The Hundred Years' War

1347–1353
The Black Death rages in Europe

1431
English burn Joan of Arc as a witch

Longbowman

Crossbowmen

▲ Bows and arrows were key weapons of the Middle Ages. Crossbows needed less strength to fire than longbows but were slower. The English longbowmen won famous victories at Crécy and Agincourt against far stronger French armies.

▼ In the 1300s, the thick walls of a besieged castle could often withstand siege weapons. In this siege of a French town the English are using early cannons. By the mid-1400s, cannons had improved; it was the increased fire power of the French artillery that helped them win the final battles of the war.

▼ As the the Hundred Years' War was being fought in Europe, a Mongol warrior Timur (or Tamerlane), who claimed to be a descendent of Genghis Khan, was building an Asian empire. Between 1379 and 1402, Timur swept south from his base at Samarkand (where he is shown being entertained) to invade Persia, India, and Turkey.

▼ Inspired by mysterious "voices," a French peasant girl, Joan of Arc, persuaded the French heir to throne, Charles, to give her troops to fight the English. In 1429, the army she led saved the city of Orléans from an English siege. It was the turning point of the Hundred Years' War. Later that year Joan stood beside Charles as he was crowned king at Rheims; by 1453 England had lost all its conquests except the port of Calais. Joan herself was captured and executed by the English. She was made a saint in 1920.

◄ *The Black Death came to Europe from Asia in 1347. It began in Italy, spreading like wildfire to the rest of the continent.*

Route of plague from Asia

SCANDINAVIA 1349

ENGLAND AND SCOTLAND 1348

NORTH RUSSIA 1349

FRANCE 1347

SOUTH RUSSIA 1345

From Asia

ITALY 1347

SPAIN 1348

OTTOMAN EMPIRE 1347

SICILY 1347

Black rat

▼ *The Black Death was bubonic plague, a type of plague carried by the fleas living on black rats. The name came from a victim's black swollen lymph nodes; the disease was usually fatal.*

THE BLACK DEATH

The Black Death was only one of the disasters to afflict Europe in the 14th century. Several bad summers and poor harvests brought starvation to many regions. Death became a frequent and familiar part of everyday life. Artists of the time depicted death in many forms, including a skeleton riding a horse.

◄ *People of the Middle Ages did not understand that disease thrives in dirt. It was usual to dump garbage onto the street and woe betide any unwary passerby!*

FURTHER FACTS

● Although the Black Death killed between one quarter and one-third of Europe's population, parts of Poland, Italy, Bohemia, and France escaped altogether. Less terrible epidemics continued for three centuries.

● At the time, people believed that cats and dogs spread the Black Death—so they killed them. As a result the true carriers, black rats, only increased.

◄ *At night, plague carts were loaded with corpses to be taken away for burial. People in towns and communities such as monasteries suffered particularly badly from the plague since closely packed areas were ideal breeding grounds for the disease-carrying rats and fleas.*

THE MODERN WORLD

The Renaissance

The 1400s and 1500s saw a period of new learning — the Renaissance — that fundamentally changed the attitudes and ideas of educated people. This renewed scholarship and the questioning of established ideas which it fostered, marks the beginning of the modern world. News of advances in philosophy, arts, and the sciences spread rapidly thanks to the development of the printed book. The new ideas also gave impetus to the Reformation — a movement that led to the division of western Christendom in the 1500s. An improved understanding of the Earth's geography encouraged Europe's seafarers and travelers to pioneer new routes in search of trade. At first European expansion hardly touched the empires of Asia but the civilizations of the Americas soon fell victim to the greed of the European invaders.

1300s
Birth of the
Renaissance in Italy

1400s–1600s
Renaissance spreads
from Italy to rest of
western Europe

1400s–1700s
Florence ruled by
the Medici family

▲ *Italy in the late 1300s was the birthplace of the Renaissance. The development of printing in Europe in the 1450s helped to spread the Renaissance to other countries.*

▶ *The new learning gave birth to humanism, a new way of thinking about human beings and their place in the universe. Humanists like the Dutch philosopher Erasmus rejected the belief that all actions are directed by God, in favor of the idea that people are responsible for their own lives.*

French chateau built
in Renaissance style

▶ *A French nobleman traveling in Italy was impressed by the new architecture. Back in France he hired an Italian architect to build him this chateau in the same style. All over Europe, people were fascinated by the ideas and designs of the Italian Renaissance and copied them in their own countries.*

Merchant and his wife
in Renaissance Italy

PATRONAGE BY POWERFUL FAMILIES

During the Renaissance, many great works of art and architecture were made possible by the patronage of rich families. In Florence the Medici, a family of merchants and bankers, were generous patrons of the arts. In Venice, the painter Vittore Carpaccio was commissioned by wealthy patrons to paint the townscapes for which he is celebrated (*left*: 'The Arrival of the Ambassadors' by Carpaccio).

▼ *The great cities of the Italian Renaissance such as Rome, Venice, Siena, and Florence (shown here), were governed as independent states. The powerful families who ruled them had become rich from banking, as well as from trading in Asia and Europe.*

▼ *Although people had used devices to tell the time for thousands of years, the first spring-driven clocks with a dial and hour hand, were not developed until the 1400s.*

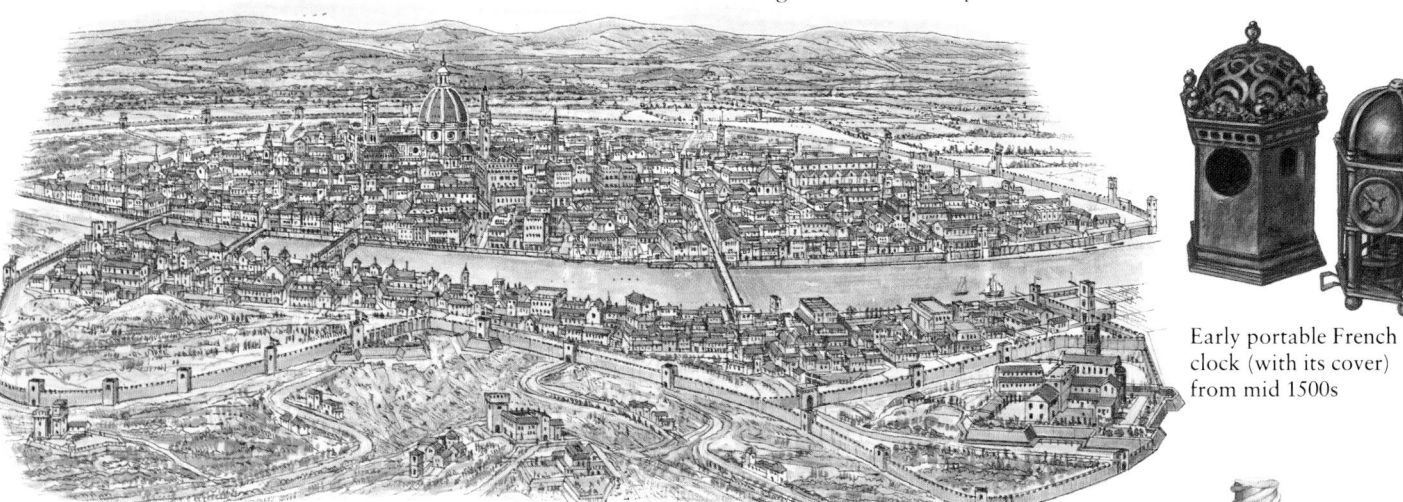

Early portable French clock (with its cover) from mid 1500s

◄ *The greatest thinkers of the Renaissance often anticipated future ideas. This sketch of a flying machine is by Leonardo da Vinci (1452–1519).*

► *The German Johannes Gutenberg introduced printing from moveable type into Europe in the 1450s. Books at once became relatively cheap and enabled the ideas of the Italian Renaissance to spread through the rest of Europe.*

THE RENAISSANCE IN EUROPE

ITALY: Brunelleschi (1377–1446), architect; Michelangelo (1475–1564), artist, architect; Galileo (1564–1642), astronomer	
FRANCE: Ronsard (1524–1585), poet; Rabelais (*c*.1494–*c*.1553), writer; Clouet (*c*.1485–1541), painter	
GERMANY: Gutenberg (*c*.1400–1468), printer; Dürer (1471–1528), painter; Holbein (*c*.1497–1543), painter	
SPAIN: Great age of Spanish exploration (*c*.1450–*c*.1550); El Greco (1541–1614), painter; Seville Cathedral (1517)	
HOLLAND/BELGIUM: Erasmus (*c*.1469–1536), philosoper; Bruegel (*c*.1525–1569), painter	
ENGLAND: Caxton (*c*.1421–*c*.1491), printer; More (1478–1535), scholar; Raleigh (*c*.1552–1618), poet, statesman	

Reformation and Counter Reformation

During the Middle Ages, Christians of western Europe belonged to a single Church, whose center was in Rome with the Pope at its head. The Reformation of the 1500s started out as an attempt to reform the Church. It grew into a movement which gave birth to a variety of Protestant Churches and led to a permanent split in the Christian community. The Counter Reformation was the attempt by the Roman Catholic Church to reform itself and win back the loyalty of those who had left it.

Protestant

Roman Catholic

Roman Catholic and Protestant

1517
Luther's criticisms begin the Reformation

1536
John Calvin founds Protestant center in Geneva

1545-1563
The Council of Trent establishes the Counter Reformation

◀ *In 1517, Martin Luther, a German monk and lecturer, nailed a list of 95 theses (statements) to the church door at Wittenberg. The theses challenged the authority of the Pope, who excommunicated Luther in 1521. His followers became known as "Protestants" because they protested against the teachings of the Roman Catholic Church.*

▶ *For nearly 40 years Europe suffered from a series of religious wars. England, Holland, and some German states fought on the Protestant side, while France and Spain supported the Roman Catholic cause. Massacres and the execution of dissenters occurred in several countries. In England many Catholics were executed in 1537, after an uprising during Henry VIII's reign.*

St. Bartholomew's Day Massacre

▶ *Years of religious conflict between Catholics and Protestants followed the Reformation. The Catholic authorities burned Protestants to death for heresy. Protestants executed Catholics, sometimes with atrocious cruelty. On St. Bartholomew's Day 1572, Catholic mobs in Paris killed about 3,000 French Protestants.*

◀ *The Reformation split Europe. The north became mainly Protestant, while southern countries remained faithful to the Church of Rome.*

◀ *The Spanish Inquisition was set up in 1478 to arrest and punish those who did not follow the Christian faith. Its first victims were Muslims and Jews. After the Reformation, it attacked all forms of Protestantism. The Inquisition executed those it found guilty in great public spectacles called* auto-da-fés.

ENGLAND BREAKS WITH ROME

In 1525, the Pope refused to let the English king, Henry VIII, have a divorce from his wife, Catherine of Aragon, so that he could marry Anne Boleyn. In order to legalize the divorce he wanted, Henry decided to take personal control of religion in England. By threats and persuasion he caused the English Parliament to pass an Act breaking all ties with the Pope in Rome. Henry then became absolute head of the Church in England.

Henry VIII and Anne Boleyn

▼ *In 1588, the English fleet defeated a large Spanish fleet, the Armada, sent by Philip II to overthrow the Protestant Elizabeth I and re-establish the Catholic faith. The Armada was defeated as much by bad weather as by the English, and only half the fleet returned to Spain. This victory helped establish the English as a major world seapower.*

Damaged Spanish galleon after the defeat of the Spanish Armada

Queen Elizabeth I

FURTHER FACTS

- In Martin Luther's time nailing theses to a church door was the recognized way of starting a debate.
- Luther's ideas were developed by a French Protestant, John Calvin, who was exiled in Geneva. Calvin's teachings were followed by Protestants in Europe and the Puritans, who later settled in America.
- The Council of Trent of 1545 began the Counter Reform movement which revived and reorganized the Catholic Church.

American Civilizations

Native Americans, or American Indians, were the first people to live in the Americas. They came to the Americas from Asia over 20,000 years ago and developed many different lifestyles. When the Spanish arrived in Central America in the 1500s, they marveled at the civilizations of the Aztecs and the Incas. They found wealthy, well-ordered cities, connected by good road systems. Far to the north, in what is now North America, people usually lived as hunters and farmers in small villages or as bands of nomadic hunters.

◄ *Between 300 and 900 the Mayans of Central America became an advanced civilization. They built massive pyramids, temples, and other structures and were the only ancient American people to develop writing and an accurate calendar.*

c.300–c.900
Mayan civilization in Central America

1400s
Aztec civilization at its height

c.1570
The Mohawk join Iroquois League

Aztec sacrificial knife

Mayan temple

▲ *A warrior tribe, the Aztecs dominated Central America in the 1400s. Their priests regularly ripped out the hearts of human beings with a sacrificial knife to please their god of war. The Incas ruled an empire in what is now Peru, South America. By the 1500s their civilization was at its peak, with great cities and beautiful works of art (below).*

Hollow wooden snake covered in turquoise

Inca silver llama

Anasazi pueblos

▶ *The Anasazi were Native Americans who lived in what is now the southwestern United States. They built villages called pueblos, where houses were joined together to form a single, large building. The Anasazi abandoned their pueblos soon after 1200, when the local climate became too dry to grow crops.*

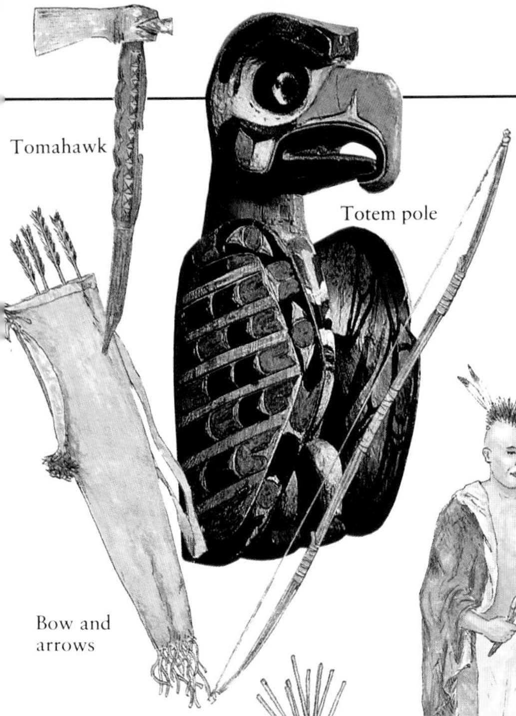

Tomahawk

Totem pole

Bow and arrows

Sioux tepee

◀ Native Americans of northwest America erected carved totem poles either as memorials to their dead, or as family records. Bows and arrows were a common weapon. The tribes of western North America developed hand axes called tomahawks.

Iroquois man and woman

▲ The Iroquois were a group of hunting tribes: the Mohawk, Oneida, Seneca, Onondaga, and Cayuga. They lived in the area that is now New York State.

Northwest Coast

ESKIMO LANDS

Far North

Plains

Eastern Woodlands

Southwest

California-Intermountain

Middle American

Caribbean

Tropical Forest

Andes—

Marginal

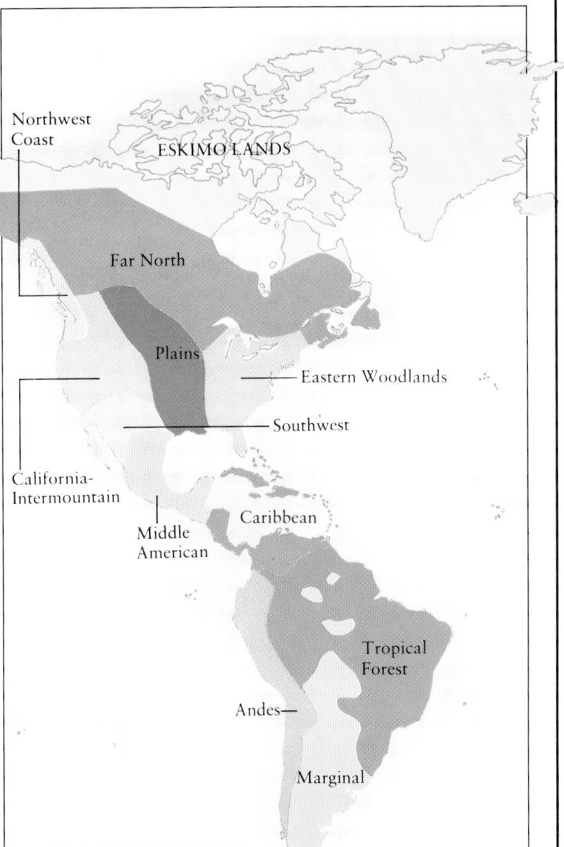

CULTURE AREAS OF NATIVE AMERICAN TRIBES

▲ The major ancient American civilizations developed in completely separate parts of the Americas over several centuries.

▲ The Sioux tribes followed the buffalo herds as they migrated across the North American Plains. Sioux shelters (tepees) were made of buffalo skins.

Mohawk village

▲ Mohawk families lived in longhouses. Their villages were surrounded by a ditch and a stockade for protection. Mohawk women grew food in plots around the houses. The men hunted deer for meat and skins. The victorious colonists destroyed the Mohawk villages in the 1700s because they had sided with the British in the Revolutionary War.

The Age of Discovery

The European navigators of the 1400s and 1500s sailed in search of profit; their discoveries were by-products of their voyages. Fortunes were to be made from the trade in ivory, jewels, perfumes, fabrics, and spices (which hid the taste of rotting food in the days before refrigeration). Many of the early voyages had a disastrous effect on the native populations. Whole tribes were slaughtered in the search for riches, or wiped out by European diseases. Not until the 1600s did some explorers seek knowledge rather than gain.

Compass

Backstaff

1271–1295
Marco Polo's travels through Asia

1492
Columbus lands in America

1768–1779
Cook explores and charts the southern Pacific

Mariner's astrolabe

THE AMERICAS
In 1492, the Italian Christopher Columbus sailed across the Atlantic from Spain to find a shorter trade route to China and India. He landed instead on Hispaniola in the Bahamas. The islanders thought the Spaniards were gods. Columbus believed that the islands were part of Asia and christened them "The Indies." Further explorations revealed the islands were not part of Asia but a totally new continent.

Columbus and islanders from Hispaniola

▲ *The simple navigation instruments of the 1400s were not very accurate. The compass, first used by the Chinese in the 1100s, was used to keep the ship on*

course. The backstaff and astrolabe helped the captain find the height of a star or the Sun so that he could work out the ship's latitude; they were difficult to use in bad weather.

Spanish caravel

▶ *The early Spanish and Portuguese voyagers chose boats called caravels for distant expeditions. Columbus's favorite ship, the* Niña, *was a caravel. She made at least five voyages to the New World. A caravel could be sailed by a 24-man crew. It was 68 ft. (21 m) long, 21 ft. (6.5 m) wide and could carry a cargo of 60 tons. Caravels were all-purpose craft. They were as dependable in ocean storms as when maneuvering in shallow water close to uncharted coasts.*

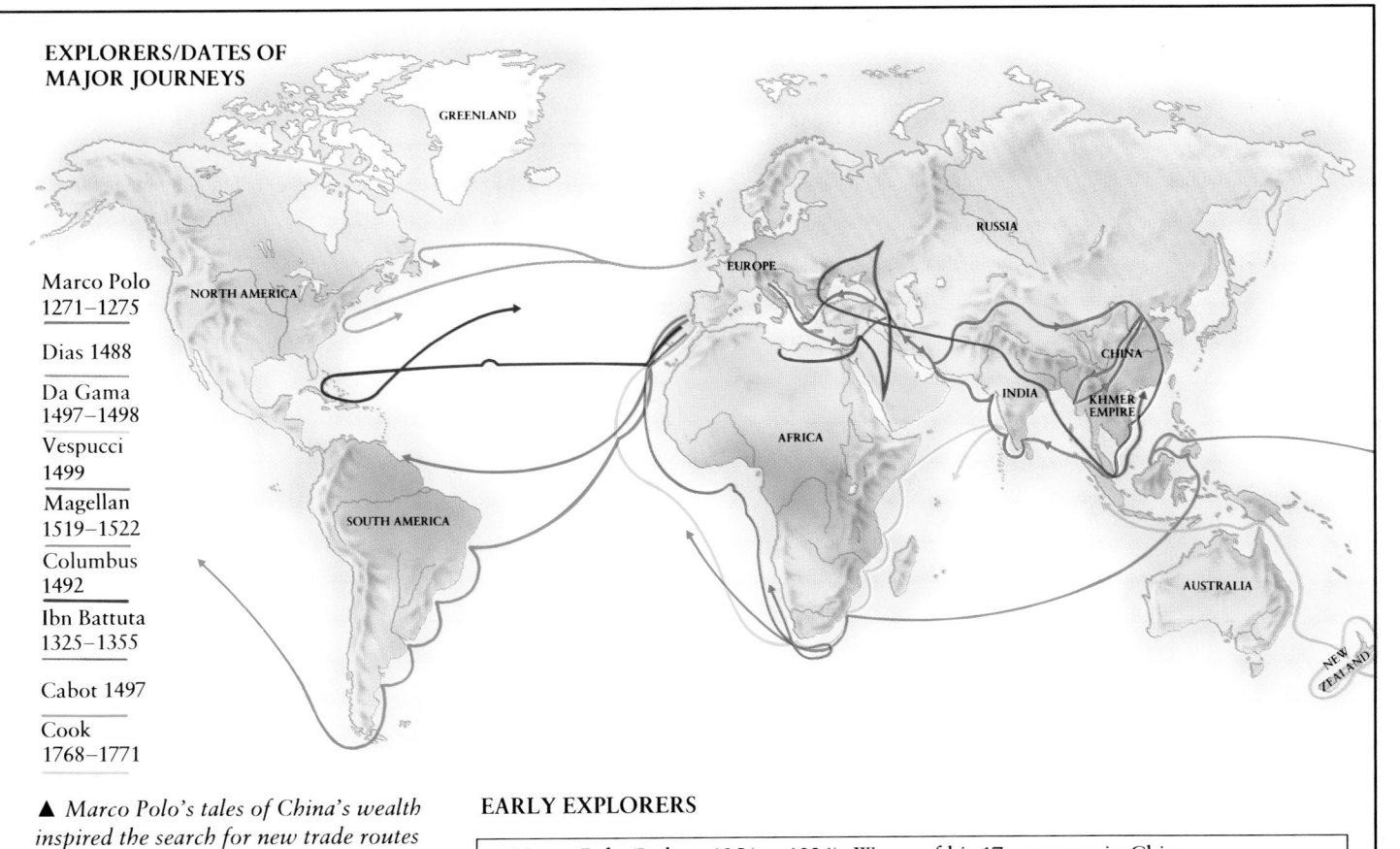

EXPLORERS/DATES OF MAJOR JOURNEYS

GREENLAND

RUSSIA

EUROPE

NORTH AMERICA

CHINA

INDIA

KHMER EMPIRE

AFRICA

SOUTH AMERICA

AUSTRALIA

NEW ZEALAND

Marco Polo 1271–1275

Dias 1488

Da Gama 1497–1498

Vespucci 1499

Magellan 1519–1522

Columbus 1492

Ibn Battuta 1325–1355

Cabot 1497

Cook 1768–1771

▲ *Marco Polo's tales of China's wealth inspired the search for new trade routes to the East. Dias and da Gama pioneered the way around Africa. Columbus and Vespucci went west and found the route blocked by an unknown continent. Magellan's expedition was the first to sail around the world.*

▼ *Europeans knew little about the South Pacific until the three scientific voyages of the English explorer Captain James Cook in the mid-1700s. He charted Australia's east coast, claiming it for Britain. He later visited New Zealand. Cook was killed in Hawaii while looking for the Northwest Passage around North America.*

EARLY EXPLORERS

Marco Polo (Italy, *c*.1254–*c*.1324): Wrote of his 17-year stay in China	
Ibn Battuta (Morocco, *c*.1304–1369): Traveled in East Africa, Arabia, China	
Bartolomeu Dias (Port., d. 1500): First European to around Cape of Good Hope	
Christopher Columbus (Italy, 1451–1506): Made four voyages to Caribbean	
Amerigo Vespucci (Italy, 1451–1512): Sailed to Caribbean and South America	
Vasco da Gama (Port., *c*.1469–1524): Pioneered eastern sea route to India	
John Cabot (Italy, 1461–1498): Sailed across North Atlantic to Canada	
Ferdinand Magellan (Port., *c*.1480–1521): Led first expedition around world	

Captain Cook with the Maoris of New Zealand

FURTHER FACTS

● When Columbus landed on Hispaniola, about 300,000 Arawaks were living there. By 1548, European diseases, murder by the Spanish, and death from work as slaves had reduced the islanders to about 500.

● The continent of America was named after Amerigo Vespucci, an Italian who sailed with the second expedition to visit northern South America in 1499.

The East: India, China, and Japan

The most popular travel book in medieval Europe was Marco Polo's account of his years of service in the court of the Mongol ruler of China, Kublai Khan. The achievements of the great Asian empires were not mere traveler's tales. Cut off from most outside contact, the Japanese developed a unique civilization of their own. Inventions as diverse as gunpowder and the magnetic compass were used in China centuries before they were known in the West. In India the Moguls ruled a great empire half the size of Europe.

1368–1644
Ming dynasty sees period of Chinese prosperity

1500s–1700s
Mogul period in India

1630s
Japanese close their country to foreigners

▲ The four great Eastern empires stretched from China, across India and Persia to the frontiers of western Europe.

THE OTTOMAN EMPIRE

For 500 years the Ottoman empire was a great Islamic world power. It was founded in northern Turkey at the end of the 1300s. As devout Muslims, the Ottomans believed it their duty to fight to defend their religion against unbelievers. In a series of jihads (holy wars), they enlarged their empire in all directions. The chief victim of Ottoman aggression was the Christian empire of Byzantium. In 1483, the Ottomans captured Constantinople; it became the capital of their empire until the 1800s. The empire reached its greatest extent under Suleiman the Magnificent. His army overran the Balkans, and only his failure to capture the Austrian capital Vienna in 1529 (below) prevented an invasion of western Europe.

▲ In 1526, the Mogul leader Babar conquered northern India and founded an empire. His grandson was the Mogul emperor Akbar, who is buried in a superb tomb at Fatehpur Sikri.

◄ The Moguls were Muslims but Akbar (seen here in battle) won the loyalty of his Indian subjects, most of whom were Hindus, by allowing them to worship in peace. Akbar was also a generous patron of writers, artists, and architects.

▼ The architectural masterpiece of the Ming empire was the capital Peking (Beijing). At its heart lay the "Forbidden City," forbidden to all except the emperor and his household.

► The Ming era of Chinese history, from the mid-1300s to mid-1600s, is renowned for its delicate blue and white porcelain.

Ming vase

CATHOLIC MISSIONARIES

Catholic missionaries arrived in the East in the 1500s. They founded a community in China which lasted until modern times. Japanese Christianity was wiped out in 1638, when 30,000 converts were massacred near Nagasaki.

Seismograph

Chinese cannon

◄ Paper, printing, guns, gunpowder, rockets, compasses, bridges made of cast iron, seed drills, seismographs, steel, umbrellas, paper money—all were invented in China long before they were first used in the West.

► From 1339 to 1573 civil war raged in Japan. In spite of the disorder, the arts flourished. The Golden Pavilion was built (1394) in Kyoto, Japan's capital city from 794 until 1868.

Shogun

Samurai warrior

▼ Japanese women practice the Tea Ceremony in the 1700s. Tea drinking is an ancient Japanese ritual; it shows the formal behavior of Japanese life.

▲ From the 1100s to the 1800s Japan was ruled by military dictators who bore the title of shogun. The samurai were the warrior class of Japan, whose code of bravery, loyalty, and honor was known as bushido.

The Colonization of America

Spaniards began to settle on the Caribbean island of Hispaniola in 1493, a year after Columbus's first landing. In 1496, a few Spanish soldiers slaughtered thousands of rebellious native Arawaks. This pattern of oppression and murder was repeated in Mexico and Peru on a far larger scale by the expeditions of the Spanish conquistadores under Cortés and Pizarro. A century later, the early colonists in New England gradually drove out groups of Native Americans in order to occupy their land.

1492-1504
Columbus's four voyages to America

1541-1542
Orellana first European to cross South America

1733
Foundation of Georgia, the last of the original 13 colonies

▶ *In 1519, Spanish soldiers led by Cortés landed in Mexico to plunder the fabled wealth of the Aztecs. Pizarro arrived in Peru in 1532 and within two years, he had overthrown the Inca empire. The first North American colonies* (opposite page) *were settled by immigrants from several European countries.*

NORTH AMERICA
AZTEC EMPIRE
• Tenochtitlán
MEXICO
• Quito
PERU
Amazon
SOUTH AMERICA
Lima •
• Machu Picchu
Cuzco
INCA EMPIRE

Route of Cortés 1519–1522

Route of Pizarro 1532–1534

Spanish empire in Americas

◀ *In 1519, the Aztec ruler Montezuma welcomed Hernán Cortés to his capital of Tenochtitlán and showered him with gifts. The early goodwill soon turned to enmity and the Spaniards besieged the city. Aztec wood and stone weapons were no match for steel swords and crossbows. By 1521 the entire Aztec empire had fallen to the Spanish.*

BRAZIL'S ORIGIN

In the 1400s Portuguese navigators traveling to India often sailed far across the Atlantic Ocean to pick up the currents that would sweep them around the Cape of Good Hope. In 1500, on one of these voyages, a fleet led by Pedro Cabral was swept too far west. They reached the coast of Brazil, which they claimed for Portugal.

▶ *In 1532, Spanish conquistadors under Francisco Pizarro kidnapped the Inca emperor Atahualpa. Pizarro's plan was to terrify the Inca army that faced his tiny band of 159 men by capturing their emperor, who was also their god. The plot worked and the Spanish soldiers then killed more than 4,000 unarmed Inca nobles. Within hours, Pizarro was master of the Inca capital, Cuzco. Atahualpa was executed in 1533.*

Spanish conquistadores capture Atahualpa

40

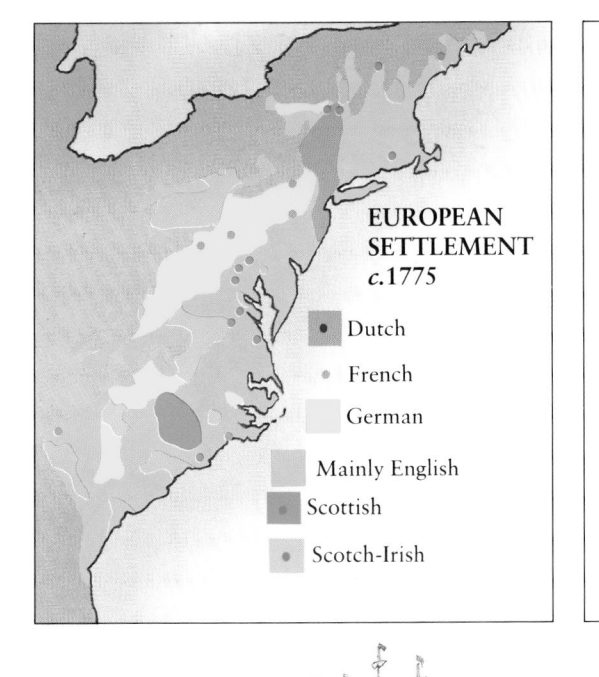

EUROPEAN SETTLEMENT *c.*1775

- Dutch
- French
- German
- Mainly English
- Scottish
- Scotch-Irish

HUDSON'S BAY COMPANY

French fur traders founded the first permanent European settlement in what is now Canada in 1604. In 1670, two French traders received the backing from a group of English noblemen to found a company to exploit the fur trade around the shores of Hudson's Bay. At the trading posts that the company set up Native Americans exchanged goods such as beaver and other animal skins for guns. After the English conquered Canada in 1763, the company gained control of the fur trade in the region.

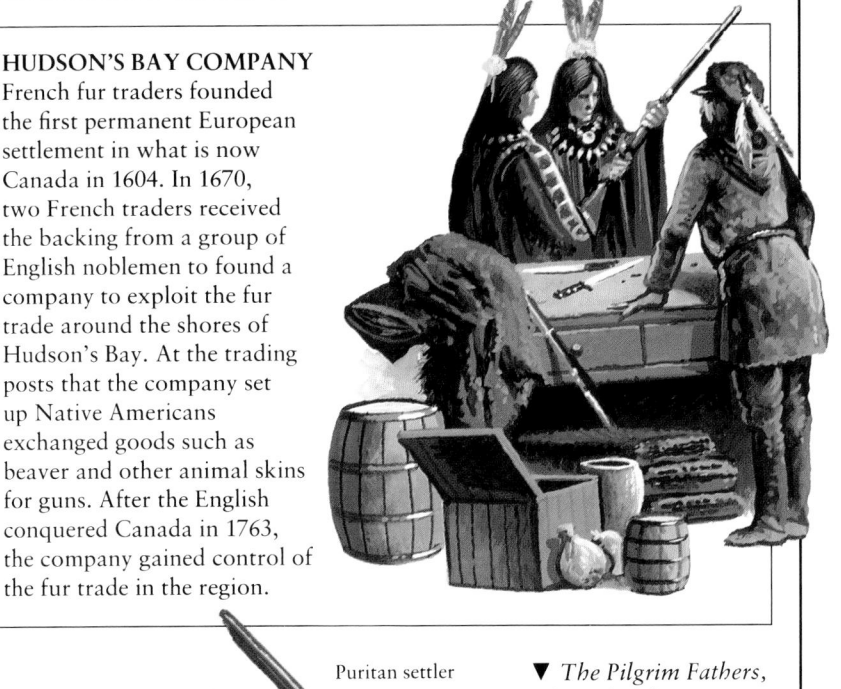

Puritan settler

▼ *The Pilgrim Fathers, who sailed from England in 1620, founded the first permanent European settlement in what is now the U.S.A. at Plymouth, Mass.*

New England farmer

New England settlement

New England woman settler

▲ *Between 1620 and 1700 about 400,000 people of European stock, most of them from England or France, were living in North America. The English arrived in far greater numbers because the area they settled in was more suitable for farming. Whole communities came out together from England. They cleared the land for cultivation and for raising farm animals. They soon produced most of the necessities of life and before long became independent of their homeland. Harvard College was founded in New England as early as 1636.*

European Society in the 1600s

At the beginning of the 1600s the newly found lands of the Americas were still a novelty to the people of Europe. Only the rich could afford its native vegetables and fruits, which later were to change the diet of much of the world. The gulf between the classes widened. The new-style houses of the wealthy were designed to afford a higher degree of comfort and luxury while the hovels of the poor remained dank, dark, and unsanitary. In England, the one place where all classes mingled was the theater.

SCIENTIFIC ADVANCES

The 1600s saw a scientific revolution with the invention of the telescope (1608), microscope (1618), thermometer (1641), and barometer (1644). Instruments such as these helped scientists gain an accurate picture of the natural world.

Englishman Isaac Newton's reflecting telescope (1668)

1582
Pope Gregory introduces modern calendar

c.1601
First performance of *Hamlet* by William Shakespeare

1665
Isaac Newton discovers force of gravity

▼ *In medieval England the ownership of land set the nobles apart from the rest of the population. But in the late 1500s rich merchants bought land as a way of becoming "gentlemen." The splendor of many of the larger houses built at this time demonstrates the growing wealth of the merchant classes.*

◀ *In most European countries, falconry was a popular sport with both kings and commoners.*

17th-century English manor house

▶ *Early visitors to America brought back many foods new to Europe, including corn, potatoes, tomatoes, and string beans. Peaches and apricots were also introduced from Asia.*

▲ *Imported cotton from the new colonies was first woven in Europe in the 1600s.*

▲ *New spices such as mace, cloves, pepper, and cinnamon were used to flavor food.*

▲ *The Spanish brought the potato to Europe, a food known in South America for 2,000 years.*

▲ *Tobacco was first used in France in the 1560s by Jean Nicot.*

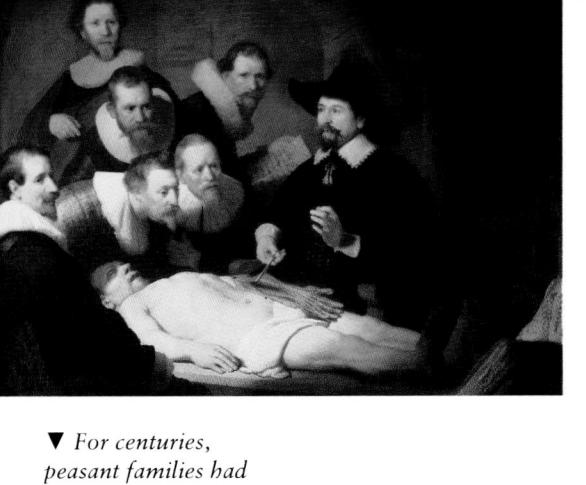

◄ *The Dutch artist Rembrandt painted* The Anatomy Lesson of Dr. Tulp *in 1642. Anatomy was then a very new science. A Belgian doctor, Andreas Vesalius, published the first accurate account of the human body's bones and nervous system in 1543.*

FURTHER FACTS

- In the 1600s the smoking of tobacco was thought to keep away the plague.
- Crops failed regularly in the years 1600–1720. The climate in Europe at that time was unusually severe and the period is known as "The Little Ice Age."
- Newspapers were started in the 1600s; among the earliest was the single-page *Antwerp Gazette* in Belgium.

▼ *For centuries, peasant families had lived in single-roomed, windowless hovels, which they shared with any animals they might possess.*

▼ *About 90 percent of the population of Europe lived on the land. It was a hard life. Wind- and water-mills, animals, and humans were the only sources of power.*

▲ *The harvest was the most important event of a peasant's year. A poor harvest meant hunger and misery.*

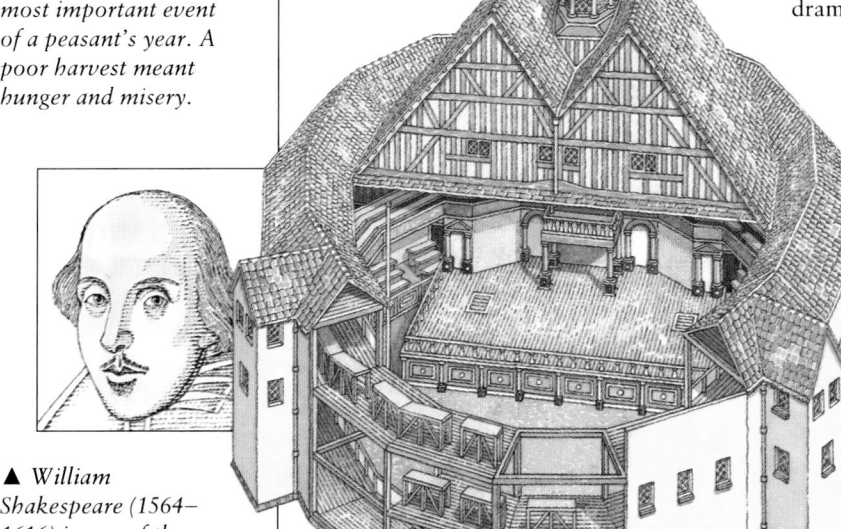

Globe theater

ELIZABETHAN DRAMA

England was the first country to produce great drama after the Reformation. By 1600, London had five theaters, some of them large enough to hold a thousand spectators. Actors, who a few years earlier had been imprisoned as "rogues and vagabonds" by the English authorities, were now patronized by Queen Elizabeth and her courtiers. The need for new plays to please the growing audiences was answered by young writers such as Marlowe, Johnson, and Middleton. The most popular dramatist of them all was William Shakespeare.

▲ *William Shakespeare (1564–1616) is one of the greatest of English-language dramatists.*

◄ *Many of Shakespeare's plays were performed at the Globe theatre, one of the first public theaters in London.*

Africa and the Slave Trade

Powerful, well-developed civilizations existed in Africa centuries before the Europeans arrived. Slavery was a recognized part of most of these societies and when the first Europeans arrived, slaves were among the goods exchanged in trade. At first, only a few slaves were taken but the number rose to millions when slaves began to be transported across the Atlantic to work on the plantations of the European colonies in America. The loss of so many people was a catastrophe for large regions of Africa.

Pre-1500s	1500s	1700s
Arabs capture and sell Africans as slaves	Europeans begin shipping slaves to New World	Height of transatlantic slave trade

GREAT ZIMBABWE

The ancient city of Great Zimbabwe lies in the modern country of Zimbabwe to which it gave its name. Prehistoric farmers were the first people to occupy Zimbabwe, but the ruins which remain today date from the middle of the 1300s. The city was then the center of a powerful empire which traded as far afield as China. The ruins of Great Zimbabwe consist of a tower, 30 ft. (9 m) high, surrounded by part of a dry stone wall, 790 ft. (240 m) around and 33 ft. (10 m) high.

▶ *The cities of Ife and Benin were the centers of two West African trading kingdoms dating from the 1200s. Both kingdoms produced superb sculptures in bronze, wood, and terracotta.*

13th-century terracotta head from Ife

FURTHER FACTS

- Denmark first made the slave trade illegal (1792); the U.S. Congress outlawed the trade in 1808. William Wilberforce led the British anti-slavery movement; the trade was abolished in Britain in 1807.
- Desperate slaves sometimes mutinied; sailors were known to hold matches near the ships' cannons as a precaution when the slaves were above deck.

Charles II guinea coin

▲ *The kingdoms of West Africa were rich in gold. Arabs called the area "Guinea" and Europeans borrowed the word. In 1663, a coin made of Guinea gold was struck in England by order of Charles II. By the mid-1600s the Guinea coast was supplying most of the New World's slaves.*

▶ *Europeans brought goods such as guns to coastal African rulers to exchange for slaves who had either been kidnapped or were prisoners of war. Many slaves did not survive the voyage to the Americas, often dying from disease or suicide. After the slaves had been landed, the ships returned to Europe with cargoes of sugar and tobacco.*

► Zanzibar Island lies off the coast of present-day Tanzania on the east coast of Africa. Once Muslims from the Middle East had conquered large parts of North Africa in the A.D. 600s and 700s, they began to travel south, to trade south of the Sahara Desert. Africans in these regions sold slaves to the Arabs along with ebony and ivory. By the time the Portuguese arrived in Africa in the 1400s the slave trade had been established for hundreds of years.

In 1698, Arabs from the Middle East captured the Portuguese trading post on Zanzibar and made it into a base for slave trading on the eastern mainland.

▼ In 1482, the Portuguese built a castle at El Mina (now in Ghana) to defend their trade with the gold mines inland. French, Dutch, and British merchants soon built their own forts on the west African coast as warehouses for the slave trade.

▼ The Slave Coast was the area between the Gold Coast (now Ghana) and the Niger River. The countries which controlled the slave trade—Britain, France, Holland—had no interest in going further into the interior of the continent. Portugal supplied slaves for Brazil from Angola.

THE GROWTH OF THE SLAVE TRADE, 1526–1810

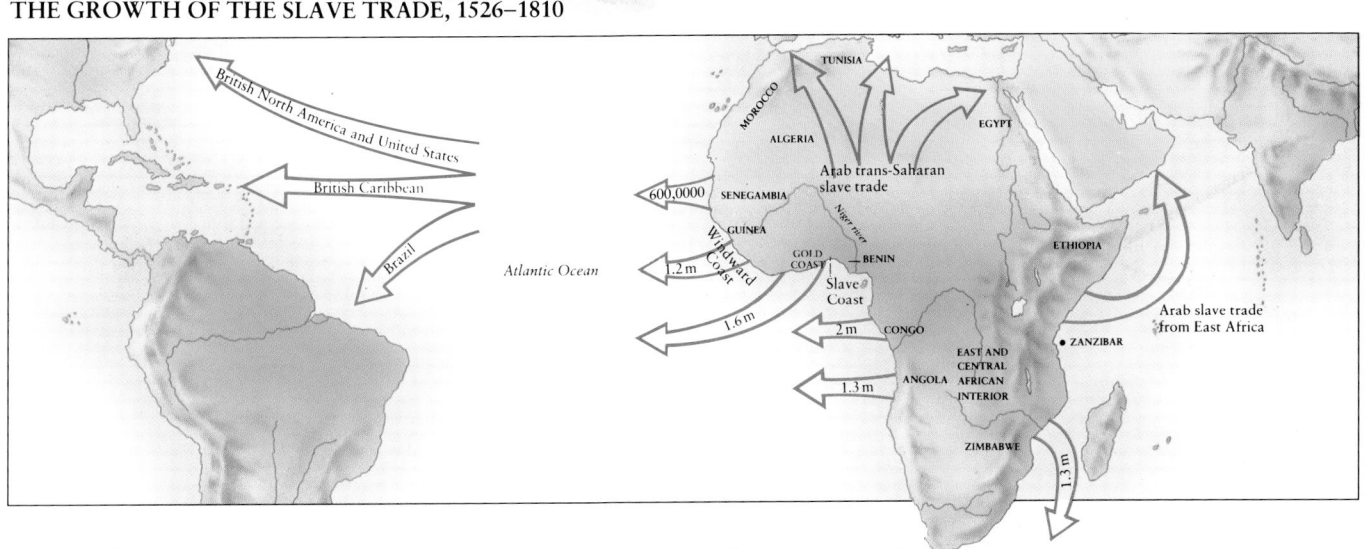

▲ Slave ships were dangerously overloaded. Slaves were often packed so tightly that they could only sit or lie flat for the long voyage to the Americas.

This painful device prevented the wearer lying down

◄ Newly captured slaves were chained together by the neck or feet and marched in long rows called "coffles" to the coast to await shipment abroad. Iron collars, sometimes with heavy weights attached, prevented slaves from running away. During the whole Atlantic crossing they were chained in the hold of the ship.

Iron manacles

THE AGE OF KINGS

Kings and Commoners

The 1600s was the age of absolute rulers. Not only in Europe, but in India, China, and Japan, power was wielded by kings, emperors, or shoguns who had total authority over their subjects. Only in England was its king, Charles I, defeated in a civil war and executed by order of parliament. In Europe the most powerful monarchs were Louis XIV of France and Peter the Great of Russia. Peter forced drastic reforms on his backward country.

Louis's reign brought the French monarchy to its zenith, even while his financial extravagance contributed to its destruction less than 70 years after his death. In India, the Moguls built mosques, tombs, citadels, and palaces of unparalleled splendor. The 1600s and 1700s also confirmed Europe's world leadership. The growth of their empires overseas was to bring nearly half the world under Europe's control.

▼ *Compared with western Europe, Russia was poor and backward when Peter the Great became tsar in 1682. Peter resolved to make Russia a great power. He toured Europe to recruit technicians and craftsmen. He reformed the government and modernized his army and navy. He also moved his capital to the new city of St. Petersburg, which he called his "window to the West."*

1643–1715	1649	1682–1725
Reign of Louis XIV of France	Charles I beheaded in England	Reign of Peter the Great of Russia

A jeweled cup given by Peter the Great to his son Alexis

Peter the Great in England

Russian boyars

▲ *The boyars were a group of families who had been the ruling class in Russia since the Middle Ages. Peter abolished their powers and ordered that their beards be cut off as a symbol of their lost authority.*

◄ *Under Peter, Russian laborers (serfs) continued to live in great poverty; in the countryside, people often starved in the harsh Russian winters.*

FURTHER FACTS

● Louis XIV's absolute control of France is epitomized by his supposed remark *"L'état, c'est moi"* ("I am the state").
● After Charles I's execution, England became a commonwealth ruled by parliament. In 1653, Oliver Cromwell, a general in the civil war, became lord protector. The monarchy was restored in 1660 when Charles II returned to England.
● A brilliant general, Cromwell was also ruthless, as shown by his forced settlement of Protestants in Catholic Ireland after Ireland rebelled against English rule in 1649.

◀ Like his father James I, Charles I of England believed he had been appointed by God to rule his country. He refused to accept parliamentary control of his policies and imposed taxes without parliament's consent. For 11 years he governed on his own. In 1642, the quarrel between king and parliament developed into a civil war. Charles was supported by the nobles, Anglicans, and Catholics. The parliamentary army was mostly made up of working men. After a series of victories by the parliamentarian general Oliver Cromwell, Charles surrendered in 1645. He was put on trial, found guilty of treason, and executed in 1649.

▼ Louis XIV built the most magnificent palace in Europe for himself and his court at Versailles, near Paris. No cost was spared, and the finest artists were hired to decorate it with sculptures, carvings, and paintings. It was surrounded by beautiful formal gardens. Versailles is considered to be the greatest architectural achievement of the 1600s.

Known as the "Sun King," Louis XIV's emblem was a golden sun

◀ A tapestry of a scene at the world-famous Gobelins workshops. Louis XIV inspects furnishings intended for Versailles. Louis and his minister Colbert encouraged the establishment of French factories to provide tapestries and other luxurious items for his palaces.

LOUIS XIV'S EXTRAVAGANCE
Louis XIV doubled taxes to raise money for both the building of his palace at Versailles and to keep France in a series of European wars. But the wars brought France no gains and Louis' extravagance created an enormous strain on the country's resources. Six out of every 10 francs collected in taxes had to pay for the building and upkeep of Versailles alone.

The Age of Reason

The Age of Reason, or Enlightenment, was a period from about 1650 to 1750 when people in western Europe believed that everything in nature could be explained by scientific enquiry and reason. This led to a questioning of established beliefs and to support for religious tolerance in much of Europe and the British North American colonies (later the United States). Even despotic rulers such as Frederick the Great of Prussia tried to put the new social and political ideas into practice in their states.

1596–1650
Life of René Descartes. The Age of Reason grew from his ideas.

1740
Prussia given freedom of press and worship by Frederick the Great.

1751–1776
Denis Diderot publishes his multivolume *Encyclopédie*.

▼ *In 1735, a Swedish doctor, Carl von Linné (known as Linnaeus), produced the first logical system for naming and classifying plants and animals. He gave everything two names. The first part of the name is the* genus *(group), the second part the* species *(kind). In 1801, the French naturalist Jean-Baptiste Lamarck devised a system for classifying animals without backbones (invertebrates).*

◀ *The baroque was the name given to the style of European art in the 1600s. Its leading artist was Rubens, whose paintings for the French court included* The Marriage of Marie de Médicis to Henri IV. *In the 1700s a renewed interest in classical art caused many public buildings in Europe to be modeled on Greek temples (below).*

Old Museum, Berlin, Germany

BALLET AND OPERA
Ballet was developed as an entertainment in the French court of the 1600s. The first public performance was in France in about 1708. The first operas were composed in Italy in the 1590s, but the art form reached greater heights in the works of Gluck and Mozart in the 1700s. Elaborate sets and costumes dazzled the audiences with spectacular effects.

Early ballet dancer

17th-century opera

▶ *Frederick II of Prussia, known as "the Great," was perhaps the outstanding monarch of the Age of Reason. Frederick was a brilliant general in war and an able administrator in times of peace. He was a keen student of literature, philosophy, and music, and played the flute almost as a professional. A talented composer himself, he was a generous patron of other composers, notably of Johann Sebastian Bach. He also corresponded with Voltaire and other leading thinkers of the time.*

Frederick the Great playing the flute

▼ *In 1675, Charles II of England founded the Royal Observatory at Greenwich, near London. Its purpose was to provide aids to accurate navigation for ships on the high seas. The Greenwich system of geographical longitude and timekeeping has since become standard throughout the world.*

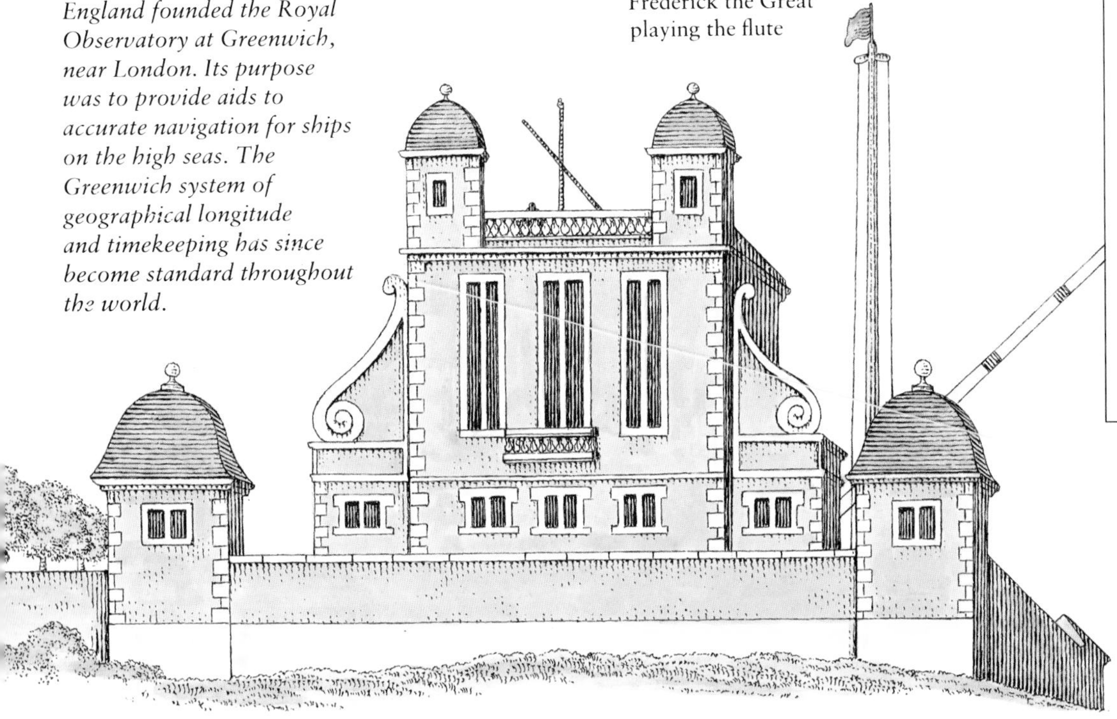

FURTHER FACTS

● Frenchman René Descartes, usually called the father of modern philosophy, was also a brilliant mathematician and scientist. Queen Kristina of Sweden hired him to give her lessons in philosophy.

● Denis Diderot's *Encyclopédie* not only condemned the monarchy in France, it also denounced the power of the Catholic Church. The French authorities banned its sale and Diderot was in constant danger of imprisonment.

● The *English Dictionary* (1747–1755), compiled by Dr Samuel Johnson, is the model for all the English-language dictionaries that have appeared since.

▼ *The great work that promoted the humanistic philosophy of the Age of Reason was the* Encyclopédie *(1747–1772), edited by a universal genius, the French philosopher Denis Diderot. The 35 volumes reviewed the arts and sciences of the time.*

Japanese porcelain figures c. 1700

JAPANESE ISOLATION

During the 1630s, Japan's rulers decided that contact with the West must end. In particular, they feared that Christian missionaries might bring European armies to invade Japan. They therefore banned most foreigners from entering Japan and the Japanese from leaving their country. As a result, people in the West were unable to appreciate the great beauty of the Japanese art of this period until the late 1800s.

European Settlement Overseas

By the beginning of the 1600s, the heyday of Portuguese and Spanish expansion had passed. It was now the French, Dutch, and British who built empires overseas. Most of their colonies were not established by governments but by groups of merchants organized into trading companies, such as the Dutch and British East India Companies. The company was granted the right to trade in the area by the local ruler. Later the trading companies were dissolved and their possessions became part of their country's empire.

New Amsterdam (later Manhattan), 1630s

1600	1641	1763
British East India Company founded	Dutch seize Malacca from Portuguese	Peace of Paris ends Seven Years' War

▲ The first Europeans to settle along the Hudson River Valley, in present-day New York state, were the Dutch. In 1625, they built a trading post on Manhattan Island which they had bought from the Native Americans. The British captured the colony in 1664 and renamed it New York.

▶ The Dutch East India Company was set up in 1602 to promote and defend Dutch trade with the East Indies. By 1641, the company had taken the place of the Portuguese as controllers of the valuable East Indian spice trade. In 1652, the company founded a base at the Cape of Good Hope as a staging post for Dutch ships on the voyage from Europe to the East Indies. This began Dutch settlement in South Africa.

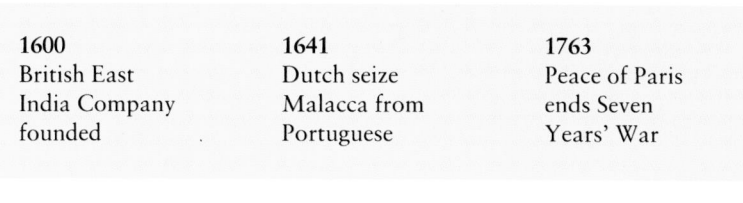

▲ Samuel de Champlain (c.1570–1635) was one of the founders of the French colonies in North America. In 1603, he explored the St. Lawrence River in Canada. In 1608, he built a fur-trading post on its shores which he called Quebec.

Dutch traders at the Cape of Good Hope in 1652

Capture of Quebec, 1759

▶ The Seven Years' War (1756-1763) involved several European powers; France and Britain were in conflict because of a longtime rivalry for colonial supremacy in India and North America. The fate of the North American colonies was decided in 1759 when a British force led by General James Wolfe captured Quebec, the capital of New France (present-day Canada). Quebec's fall made sure that Britain gained all of France's lands in North America.

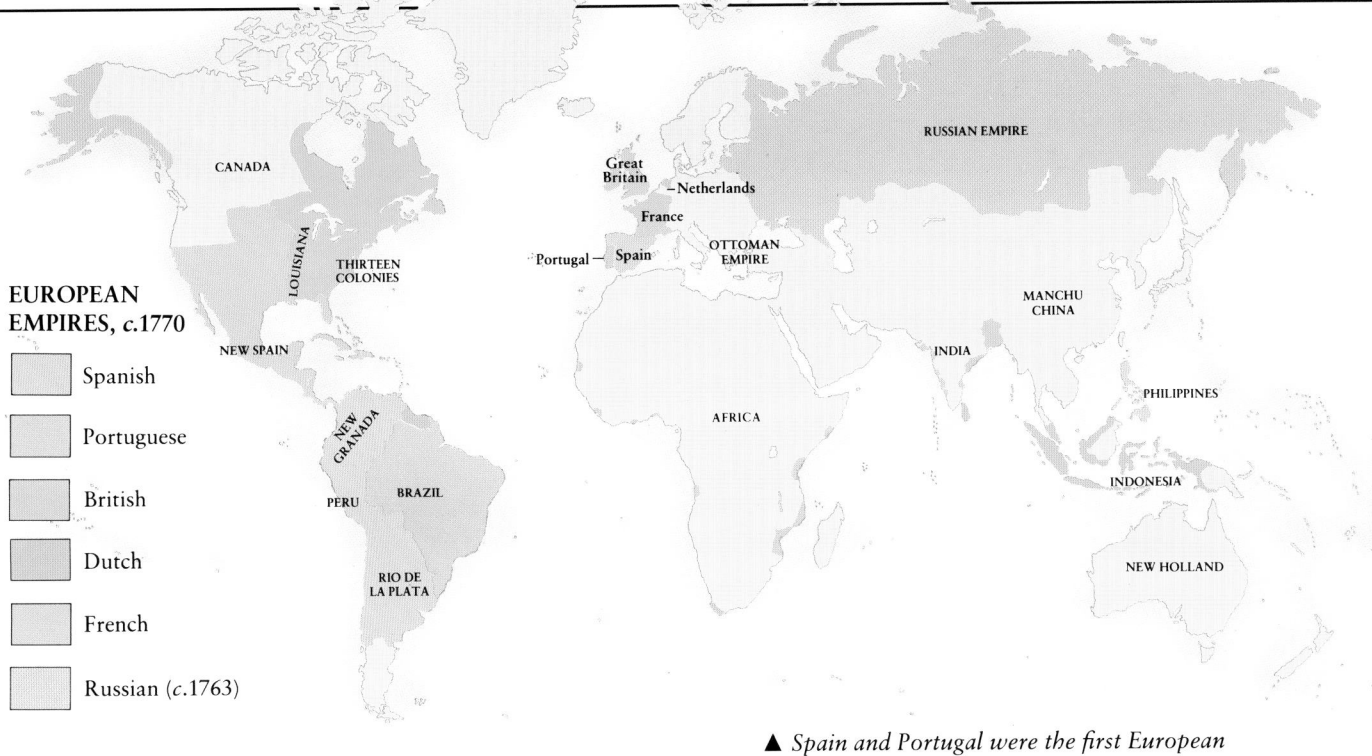

EUROPEAN EMPIRES, c.1770

- Spanish
- Portuguese
- British
- Dutch
- French
- Russian (c.1763)

CANADA
LOUISIANA
THIRTEEN COLONIES
NEW SPAIN
NEW GRANADA
PERU
BRAZIL
RIO DE LA PLATA

Great Britain
Netherlands
France
Portugal — Spain
OTTOMAN EMPIRE
RUSSIAN EMPIRE
MANCHU CHINA
INDIA
AFRICA
PHILIPPINES
INDONESIA
NEW HOLLAND

▲ Spain and Portugal were the first European countries to build empires overseas. The Portuguese focused their efforts on Africa and Asia. The Spanish occupied all of South America except for Brazil. The English and French settled in North America. Dutch traders colonized the East Indies.

Musketeers aboard the British warship Centurion, 1752

▶ During the 1700s, European colonial powers were frequently at war with each other. Since the colonies could only be reached by ship, many clashes took place at sea. A major objective in war was to interfere with the enemy's trade and to seize enemy ships. Here, British musketeers on the warship Centurion fire on the Covadonga, loaded with silver from the Spanish colony of Mexico.

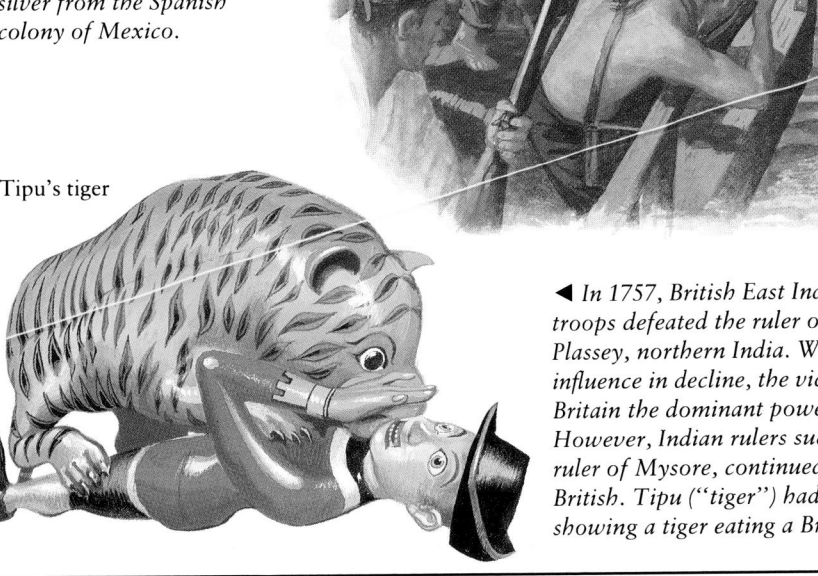

Tipu's tiger

◀ In 1757, British East India Company troops defeated the ruler of Bengal at Plassey, northern India. With French influence in decline, the victory made Britain the dominant power in India. However, Indian rulers such as Tipu, ruler of Mysore, continued to defy the British. Tipu ("tiger") had a model made showing a tiger eating a British soldier.

FURTHER FACTS

- In the 1600s and 1700s the term "East Indies" was originally used to describe India; later it came to refer to southeast Asia, especially Indonesia.
- The only country in Asia never to be colonized by any European power was Siam (now Thailand).
- In 1756, a number of British prisoners were shut up in a small room during a battle between British and Indian troops. Several died in the suffocating heat. The British greatly exaggerated the smallness of the room and the number of deaths. The incident became known among them as "The Black Hole of Calcutta."

51

THE AGE OF REVOLUTIONS

The American Revolutionary War

The colonists of the Thirteen Colonies of British North America were governed from London. They were treated as British subjects except that they did not have the vote and therefore nobody to represent their interests in parliament. When parliament passed laws which imposed new taxes, the colonies rebelled. In the revolution that followed the colonists won their independence from Britain and set up a republic. The success of the Americans in overthrowing a ruling authority was an inspiration to the peoples of Europe who lived under repressive regimes. Within a few years of the Americans' revolution, the French had risen against their king and ruling classes. After several years of violence and bloodshed they established a republic which in its turn became the model for revolutionaries throughout the world.

1775-1776
Early fighting around Boston

Sept. 1777
Americans win key battle of Saratoga

Sept. 1783
Britain recognizes independence of the United States

◀ *The "Boston Tea Party" was a protest against taxation in Britain's North American colonies. The colonists objected to paying taxes on items such as tea, imposed by the British parliament without their consent. A small band of colonists dressed up as Mohawk Indians, boarded three ships in Boston harbor and dumped tea chests in the sea. The British reacted with a series of punitive laws known as the "Intolerable Acts," which included the closure of the port of Boston until money was paid to the East India Company for the loss of the tea.*

▶ *The Declaration of Independence, adopted on July 4 1776, is the foundation document of the United States of America. It proclaimed the separation of the American colonies (which now became states) from Britain. The lawyer, Thomas Jefferson (center), was the principal author. The document was signed by 56 delegates of the Thirteen Colonies. Since 1776, July 4 has been celebrated as a national holiday.*

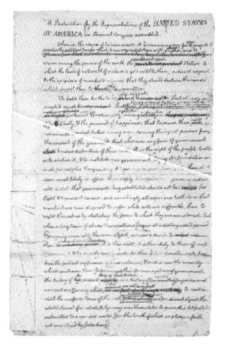

The Liberty Bell in Philadelphia is a symbol of American independence

Draft of the Declaration of Independence

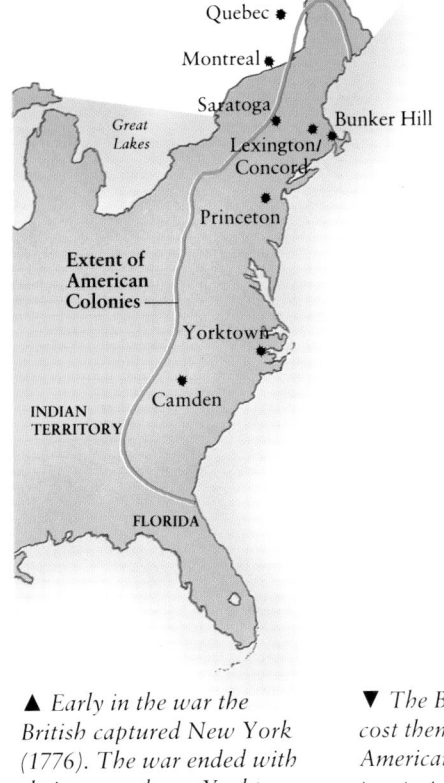

Quebec

Montreal

Saratoga

Great Lakes

Lexington/Concord

Bunker Hill

Princeton

Extent of American Colonies

Yorktown

INDIAN TERRITORY

Camden

FLORIDA

▲ *George Washington became commander of the American forces in 1775. On Christmas night, 1776, Washington crossed the Delaware River, before beating the British in the* battles of Trenton and Princeton. Washington's greatest achievement was to keep 16,000 volunteer troops together during five years of conflict in which they suffered many reverses.

▲ *Early in the war the British captured New York (1776). The war ended with their surrender at Yorktown (1781). A turning point was the American alliance with the French in 1778.*

▼ *The British victory at Bunker Hill (1775) cost them 1,000 casualties against 400 American casualties. Their well-drilled troops trained for European wars stood in closely packed ranks firing volleys of shot in the direction of the enemy. The Americans, used to killing game and fighting on the frontiers with Native Americans, were skilled marksmen who could put a bullet through a man's head at 200 paces.*

American revolutionary soldier

British grenadier *c.* 1775

KEY DATES

● **April 1775:** The first shots of the war were fired at Lexington near Boston, when British troops arrived to destroy the arms store of the local militia.

● **June 1775:** George Washington becomes commander of the rebel American army.

● **March 1776:** The British evacuate Boston.

● **July 4 1776:** The Declaration of Independence is adopted by delegates of the 13 Colonies.

● **October 1781:** The British are besieged at Yorktown by the Americans and their French allies.

● **September 1783:** U.S. and Britain sign final peace treaty in Paris.

The French Revolution

The revolution in France of 1789 is one of the most important events in human history. It is important because it overthrew a powerful monarchy and introduced new principles of democratic government. The revolution was extremely violent, killing both the French king and thousands of citizens. France was in chaos as one group of revolutionaries after another failed to establish firm government. Eventually, the French army seized power, led by the great and ambitious general, Napoleon Bonaparte.

July 1789
Mobs storm the Bastille; the revolution begins

July 1794
Robespierre executed; the Terror ends

November 1799
Napoleon overthrows the revolutionary government

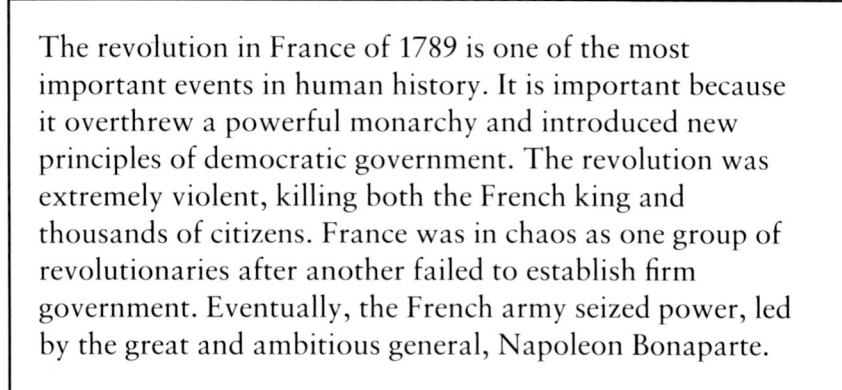

▲ *Louis XVI was shy and weak rather than bad or cruel. He preferred hunting to governing his country. He was also unfortunate in having an unpopular wife, the pleasure-loving Marie Antoinette. In 1793, he was to pay with his life for his indifference to the misery that heavy taxation was causing ordinary French people.*

▲ *By 1789, the States-General (a national parliament) had not met since 1614. In June, the Third Estate (the commoners in the parliament) met in a tennis court where they took an oath not to disband until France had a new assembly and constitution. The Tennis Court Oath was the beginning of the revolution.*

▶ *Although Louis XVI gave in to the Third Estate and ordered that a new National Assembly should meet, rumors spread through Paris that the king would soon disband it. The rumors started riots both outside Paris and in the city itself, where on 14 July an angry mob captured the Bastille prison, a symbol to Parisians of royal power.*

◀ *In 1789, many working men and women in Paris were jobless and hungry. On July 14 the price of bread was doubled. The unemployed joined shopkeepers and workers to form the mob that stormed the Bastille.*

Woman revolutionary with tricolor rosette in her hat

Revolutionaries were called *sans culottes* because they wore pants rather than breeches (unlike the nobility)

KEY DATES

● **1789:** France was divided by law into three groups called Estates. The First Estate was the clergy; the Second Estate, the nobility; the Third Estate, the commons (town corporations).
● **June 1789:** The Tennis Court Oath.
● **June 1791:** The royal family is caught trying to leave France and brought back to Paris.
● **January 1793:** The king, Louis XVI, executed. His queen, Marie Antoinette, was guillotined in October 1793.
● **September 1793–July 1794:** Reign of Terror; ends with death of Robespierre.
● **1795–1799:** France ruled by a five-member Directory.

UNITÉ
INDIVISIBILITÉ
DE LA
RÉPUBLIQUE
LIBERTÉ
ÉGALITÉ
FRATERNITÉ
OU LA
MORT

TERREUR

RÉPUBLICAINS

▶ *Slogans such as "unity, liberty, equality, and fraternity—or death" were seen on the revolutionary posters stuck up in Paris.*

◀ *The period from mid-1793 to mid-1794 is called the Terror. France was then ruled by the Jacobins, a group of extremist revolutionaries led by Maximilian Robespierre. The Jacobins ruled by fear. Thousands of innocent people from all classes were condemned for their opposition to the revolution. Large crowds watched the public executions on the guillotine.*

Napoleon Bonaparte

Napoleon Bonaparte seized power in France when the government turned to the army for support. Napoleon was the army's most successful general. From 1799, Napoleon led a number of brilliant military campaigns that won him control of most of western Europe. His one major defeat was at Trafalgar in 1805, which gave Britain command of the seas. From 1812, Napoleon's fortunes declined. His armies retreated from Russia and he lost a series of battles in Germany. His defeat at Waterloo in 1815 ended his career.

1799
Napoleon becomes first consul of France

1812
French army retreats from Russia

1815
Napoleon finally beaten at battle of Waterloo

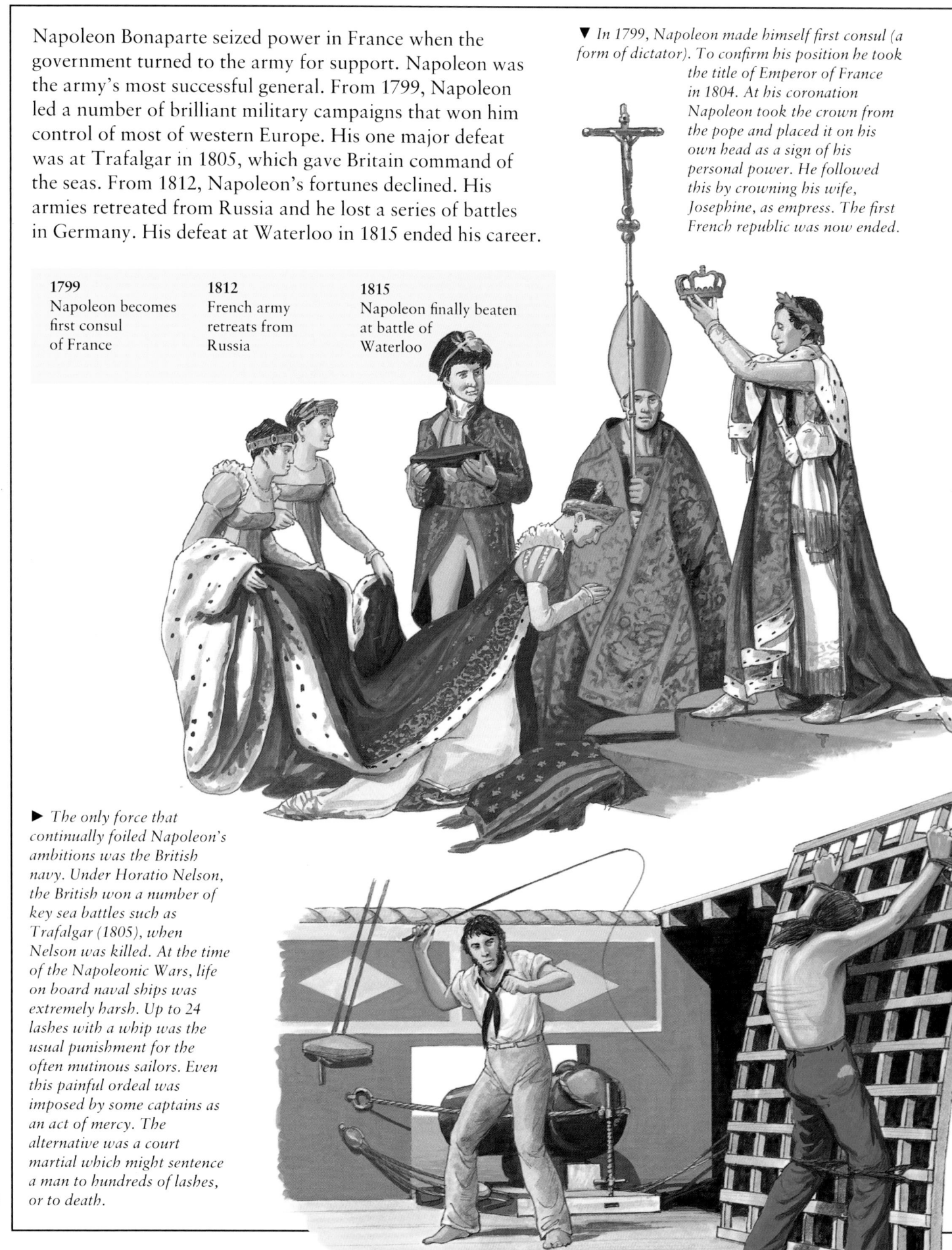

▼ *In 1799, Napoleon made himself first consul (a form of dictator). To confirm his position he took the title of Emperor of France in 1804. At his coronation Napoleon took the crown from the pope and placed it on his own head as a sign of his personal power. He followed this by crowning his wife, Josephine, as empress. The first French republic was now ended.*

▶ *The only force that continually foiled Napoleon's ambitions was the British navy. Under Horatio Nelson, the British won a number of key sea battles such as Trafalgar (1805), when Nelson was killed. At the time of the Napoleonic Wars, life on board naval ships was extremely harsh. Up to 24 lashes with a whip was the usual punishment for the often mutinous sailors. Even this painful ordeal was imposed by some captains as an act of mercy. The alternative was a court martial which might sentence a man to hundreds of lashes, or to death.*

▲ One of Napoleon's most famous battles was in 1807 at Eylau, now in Poland, when in a snowstorm his army withstood heavy losses to hold off a far larger Russian army.

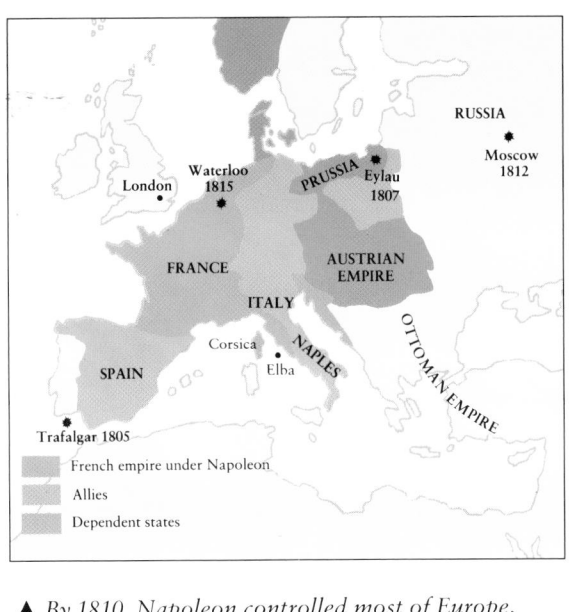

▲ By 1810, Napoleon controlled most of Europe, including several German states and much of Poland. He made members of his family the rulers of Spain, Italy, and the Netherlands.

FURTHER FACTS

● By destroying the joint Franco-Spanish fleet at Trafalgar in 1805, the British navy saved Britain from invasion.

● In 1814, Napoleon was defeated by the armies of a European coalition at Leipzig. He abdicated and was exiled on the island of Elba. In March 1815, he escaped from Elba and raised a new army. He was finally defeated by the British and Prussians at the battle of Waterloo in June 1815.

▲ In 1812, Napoleon made the disastrous decision to invade Russia; the Russians were his only remaining rivals on mainland Europe. His army reached Moscow in September 1812 to find that the Russians had burned it down. The French army was not equipped to survive the harsh Russian winter which was just beginning. Napoleon ordered a withdrawal. As the French retreated, three-fourths of the 500,000-strong army were killed by the Russians, or died of cold and hunger.

▲ After his final defeat at Waterloo, Napoleon gave himself up to the British to escape being executed by the Prussians. The British sent him to the remote Atlantic island of St. Helena, where he died in 1821.

THE AGE OF IMPERIALISM

The Industrial Revolution

The Industrial Revolution is a term describing major changes in the economic and social structure of many western countries in the 1700s and 1800s. At the beginning of the 1700s most of Europe's people lived and worked on the land. By the time the 1800s ended, most Europeans were city dwellers, earning a living in factories or offices. As work became unavailable on the land, huge numbers of Europeans migrated overseas, particularly to America. The political map of Europe was also redrawn during this period. Revolutions convulsed the continent from the 1820s to the 1870s. They swept away states ruled by hereditary families and replaced them with new nations based on shared history, culture, and language. The European powers also strove to win new colonial territories in Africa and to extend their empires in Asia and the Pacific.

1787	1789–1815	1833
In U.S. John Fitch demonstrates first workable steamboat	France's industrial revolution stopped by revolution and wars	British Factory Act bans children under nine working in factories

THE FIRST INDUSTRIAL REVOLUTION
Britain's industrial revolution was the period (1750–1850) when Britain's dominance of overseas markets through its empire, and the availability at home of coal and iron ore, transformed it from a farming to a manufacturing community. The harnessing of steam power and major new inventions led to cheap mass-manufacture of materials such as cotton. Iron, made by the new processes, was strong enough for building structures like bridges in a different way.

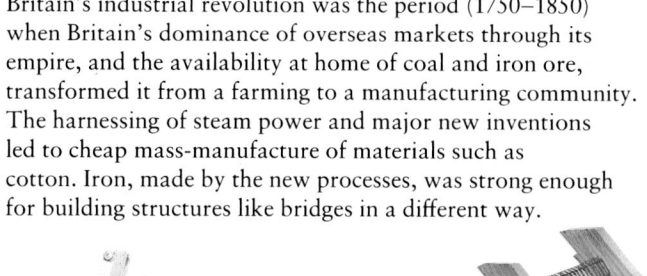

The world's first iron bridge, built in England, 1777

► *The transitions of Britain's industrial revolution were repeated elsewhere as other western countries became industrialized. Farmworkers moved to the towns, seeking work in the new factories. The densely packed, low-quality houses built for them soon became unhealthy slums.*

New factory

Workers' housing

Eli Whitney's cotton gin

Canal

Canal barge

► *In Britain, a system of canals linking the major rivers was built, providing the cheap transport the new factories needed to deliver raw materials and take away finished goods. The goods were loaded onto barges pulled by horses along tracks called towpaths. Canal-building reached its peak in Britain in the 1790s. Later in the Industrial Revolution, goods could be moved more easily on the newly built railroads.*

◄ *Before the new machines led to manufacture in factories, cloth was made in homes. Women and children did the spinning. Weaving was traditionally men's work.*

▼ *George Stephenson opened the first public railroad in Britain in 1825. In 1835, his son Robert built the engine for the first German train, Der Adler (The Eagle).*

► *In the early 1800s, children as young as five years old worked underground in the mines. They often had to work shifts of 12 hours and more. Some toiled half-naked, chained to carts laden with coal which they pulled along dark passageways. Factories also used children. The usual shift was 15 hours a day. Many children were orphans; they lived in crowded, dirty hostels where the death rate could reach 60 percent.*

▼ *In the 1700s, a revolution also took place in British farming. Jethro Tull's seed drill and improved plows raised the standard of cultivation. Animals that in an earlier age would have been slaughtered in the winter were now kept alive on root crops. Between 1700 and 1800, the yield of wheat doubled. Selective breeding meant larger, healthier livestock.*

Jethro Tull's seed drill

Improved cattle and sheep

FURTHER FACTS

● Hargreaves introduced his 8-thread spinning machine, (called "jenny" after his wife) in 1764. A later model was able to spin 120 threads.
● After Britain, the next western country to become industrialized was Belgium.
● By the 1840s France, Germany, Belgium, and the U.S. had all begun to build railroads; the coming of the railroads revolutionized travel since ordinary people were able to move about more easily.
● Towns grew rapidly: in Britain, in 1801, Manchester's population was 75,000. By 1851, it was 303,000.

The New Nationalism

Napoleon's domination of Europe at the beginning of the 1800s created a renewed desire for liberty and the pride in nationality which had inspired the French Revolution. Greece and Belgium were the first to throw off the old order and gain independence. In South America, after twenty years of uprisings and wars, independent states replaced the old empires of Spain and Portugal. By the 1870s, both Italy and Germany had become unified, and Germany had become a major new world power.

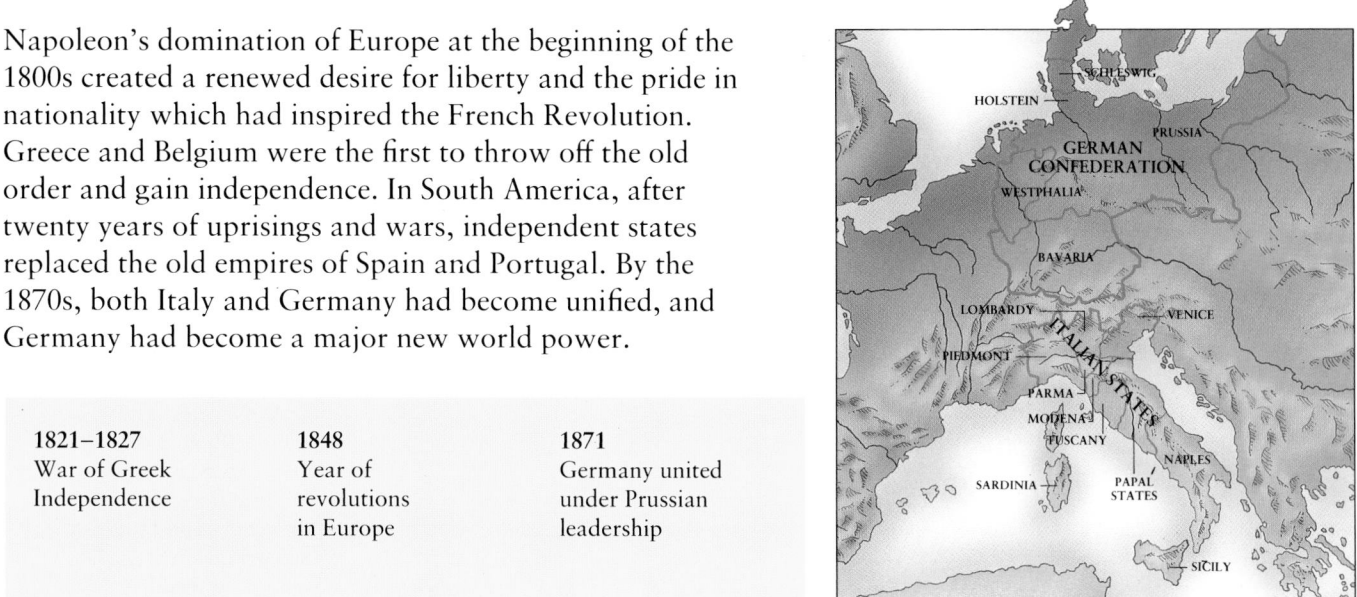

1821–1827
War of Greek
Independence

1848
Year of
revolutions
in Europe

1871
Germany united
under Prussian
leadership

▶ *The Ottoman Turks had conquered Greece in the 1500s, but the Greeks never forgot they were a nation. In 1821, they rebelled against Turkish rule. In 1827, Russia, Britain, and France agreed to use force if necessary to help the Greeks gain their independence. When Turkey refused to give up control of Greece, a joint French, Russian, and British force defeated the Turkish fleet in Navarino Bay. The battle helped Greece become independent in 1832.*

19th-century
Greek soldier

Battle of Navarino

Garibaldi embarks for Sicily

◀ *Giuseppe Garibaldi was the hero of the Italian Risorgimento – the movement to replace Austrian and French rule with unification and independence. In May 1860, he landed in Sicily with a thousand red-shirted followers. In August he crossed to the mainland and captured Naples. Garibaldi's example inspired his fellow patriots to continue the struggle which was finally won when Rome became the capital of a united Italy in 1870.*

◀ In Europe, 1848 was a year of revolutions. There were revolts in Germany, Italy, Poland, and Hungary. The rulers of France and Austria gave up their thrones after major uprisings.

▼ In July 1870, France went to war with Prussia, the leading state of Germany. The war was a disaster for France. Her armies were destroyed and Paris was under siege. The city's defenders held out for four months but in January starvation forced them to surrender. The victory united the German states. In 1871, King Wilhelm of Prussia became emperor of all Germany.

The Arc de Triomphe is protected as Parisians leave before the 1870 siege

KARL MARX

The ideas of the German philosopher Karl Marx inspired the worldwide communist movements of the 1900s. He wanted all political power to belong to the working class. Most of his writing and research was done in London, where he lived in exile from 1849. His most important works were the *Communist Manifesto* (published in Paris during the 1848 Revolution) and *Das Kapital*.

Simón Bolívar

INDEPENDENCE IN SOUTH AMERICA

The peoples of the Spanish South American empire were inspired by the French Revolution to fight for their freedom. Mexico won independence in 1821. Simón Bolívar's armies fought for the independence of Colombia and Bolivia. José San Martín liberated Chile and, with Bolívar, freed Colombia and Ecuador.

MEXICO 1821

CENTRAL AMERICAN FEDERATION 1821–1838

VENEZUELA 1830

British
Dutch
French colonies in Guyana

COLOMBIA 1819

ECUADOR 1830

BRAZIL 1822

PERU 1821

BOLIVIA 1825

PARAGUAY 1811

CHILE 1818

URUGUAY 1828

ARGENTINA 1810

FURTHER FACTS

● In 1830, the French deposed their king, Charles X. Louis Philippe became king until the 1848 revolution.

● The 1830 French uprising encouraged the Belgians to rebel against their Dutch rulers. Belgium became independent in 1833.

● In 1830 and 1863 Polish patriots rebelled against Russian rule. Both uprisings failed and many Poles were exiled to Siberia.

The American Civil War

In 1861, seven (later eleven) southern states of the U.S.A. declared themselves a separate nation: the Confederate States of America. The northern (Union) states then went to war with the South to preserve the country's unity. One important difference between the two areas was slavery. The agricultural South wished to retain it; the industrial North was determined to end it. The South lost the war because, despite early military success, it was overwhelmed by the superior forces and industrial might of the North.

1860
Abraham Lincoln elected United States president

1865
The Union wins the American Civil War

1869
First American transcontinental railroad completed

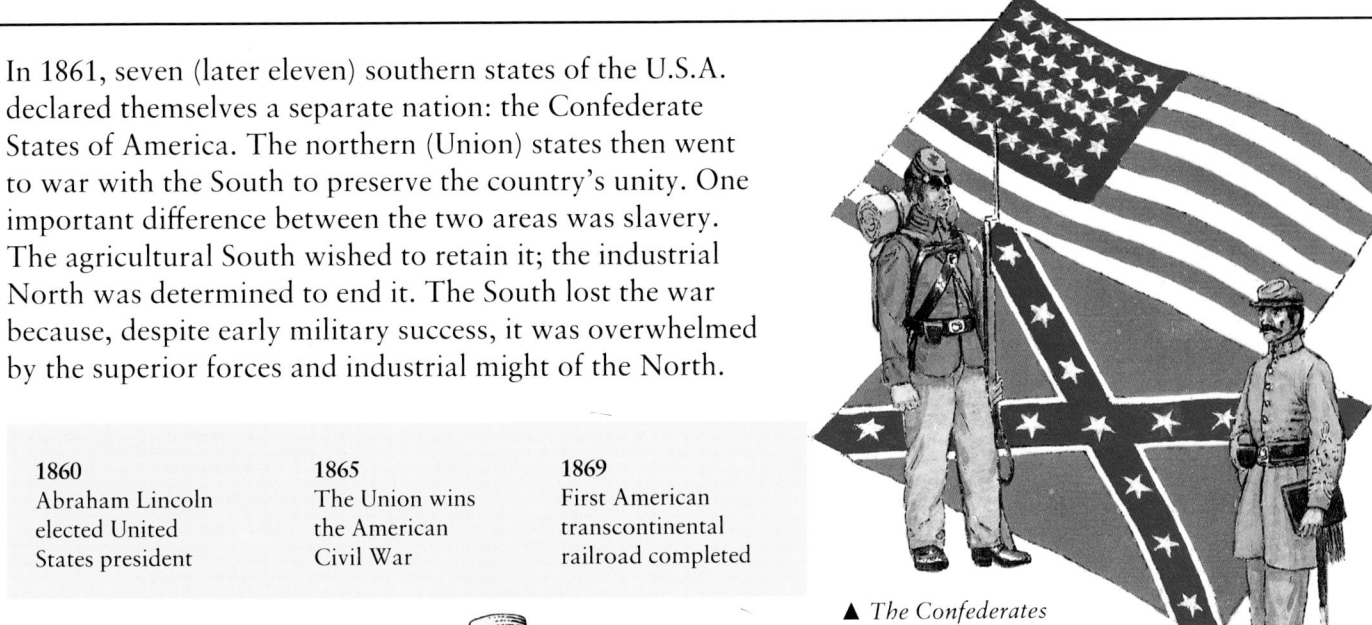

▲ *The Confederates rejected the Stars and Stripes and adopted their own flag. Their troops wore gray uniforms. The Union troops wore blue.*

Abraham Lincoln in 1861

Slaves picking cotton

◄ *The economy of the southern states was based on black slave labor. The new president, Abraham Lincoln, and his Republican party wanted to limit slavery. Afraid of being outvoted by northern non-slave states, the southern states under Jefferson Davis left the Union. War broke out in April 1861.*

▼ *New, more effective, long-range guns made the American Civil War one of the bloodiest wars in history. Three million men fought in it and over 600,000 died. However, twice as many died from disease as were killed in action.*

▶ *The division of the United States at the beginning of the Civil War. The Civil War took place over a vast area. For the first time in history, railroads played a vital part in warfare by moving troops and supplies quickly over great distances.*

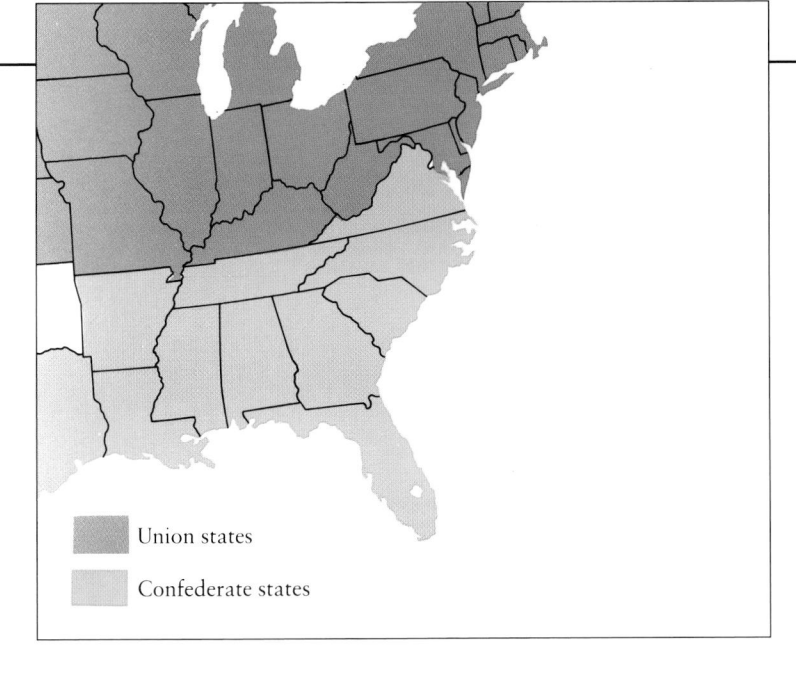

Union states

Confederate states

FURTHER FACTS

● America's first railroad opened in South Carolina in 1830.
● The Civil War began in April 1861, when Confederate artillery fired on Union troops at Fort Sumter. It ended in April 1865, when the Confederates surrendered at Appomattox, Virginia.
● A major turning point of the Civil War was the Union victory at Gettysburg, Pennsylvania in July 1863; the South then abandoned its hopes of invading the Union.
● The coming of the transcontinental railroad helped to decimate the buffalo herds on which the Plains tribes depended. By 1900, the tribes had been forcibly moved to reservations.

WINNING THE WEST

In 1803, the United States bought France's claim to the lands west of the Mississippi River for $15 million and so doubled the new country's size. The purchase of this new land began a movement to the western territories of thousands of people, seeking their fortunes and a better life. The move west increased after the Civil War in the 1860s. But the land was not empty. Native American tribes had lived on the Plains for many generations. The new settlers found they could only build and farm there if they first drove the local tribes away.

Wagon train, traveling to American West

SETTLER TRAILS ACROSS THE U.S.A.

CANADA

California

Utah

New Mexico

Pennsylvania

Texas

Georgia

Louisiana

MEXICO

▶ *The first American railroad was opened in 1830. By 1880, America's rail network exceeded that of Europe. Rail transport overcame the great distances which had hindered the development of America. It made sending goods to markets cheap and easy. In return it brought back the factory-made equipment that the Midwestern farmers needed.*

The Movement of Peoples

European migration to America gathered pace after the American Revolution. During the 1800s, millions more crossed the Atlantic. Driven out by famine, the numbers of Irish emigrants overtook those from the rest of Britain. More emigrants came from Germany and Sweden and, later, Italy, Russia, and eastern Europe. In its early years Australia had been a British prison colony. The discovery of gold in the mid-1800s increased the flow of people to both Australia and North America.

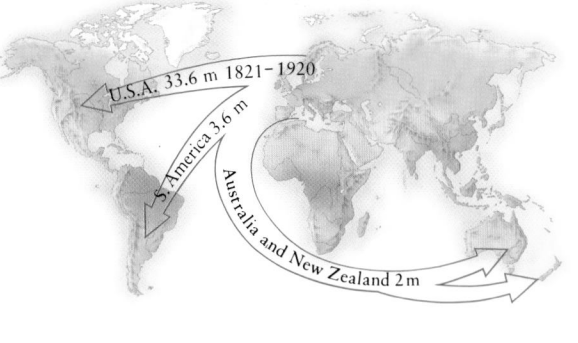

EMIGRATION FROM EUROPE, 1820s–1920s

U.S.A. 33.6 m 1821–1920

S. America 3.6 m

Australia and New Zealand 2m

1815–1914	1840s	1867
Main period of European migration	Potato famine begins	Britain ends transportation to Australia

▲ Most of the Europeans who emigrated during the 1800s went to the United States. Other favored destinations were Australia and New Zealand and the countries of South America.

Sydney Harbour in the early 1800s

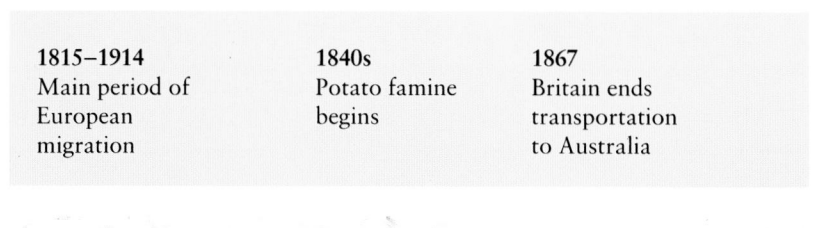

A CONVICT SETTLEMENT
In the 1700s, convicted criminals in Britain were sometimes sentenced to hard labor in its colonies overseas. Most went to North America. After the U.S. declared independence in 1776, Britain established a new penal colony at Botany Bay in Australia. Convicts were shipped to parts of Australia until the 1860s.

▲ New South Wales in eastern Australia was founded as a British prison colony. A group of convicts and guards arrived on the site of the future city of Sydney in 1788. Before then the people who lived there were Aborigines. From the 1820s, free settlers were allowed to immigrate. The rearing of sheep in the rich pastures near the coasts created a profitable wool industry. By 1900, Sydney had a population of 400,000.

Prospector panning for gold

FURTHER FACTS

- A penal colony was established on the island of Tasmania off the coast of mainland Australia in 1803; 65,000 convicts served their sentences there.
- By the 1870s, every one of the Australian Aborigines who had lived on the island of Tasmania was dead. Some had perished from European diseases; white settlers had murdered the rest.
- European immigration into the U.S. was at its height during 1901–1910, with 8,795,386 people admitted. Of those, over 6 million came from southern and eastern Europe.

◄ *In 1848, gold was discovered in California. Within a few months a gold rush had started. The nearest port, San Francisco, grew from a small town to a city of 25,000 as prospectors and other people massed to seek their fortune. In the late 1800s, there were also gold rushes in Canada, South Africa, New Zealand, and Australia.*

► *Dawson, in northeastern Canada, was typical of the towns that sprang up almost overnight in the newly discovered gold fields. At the height of the gold rush in the Yukon in the 1890s Dawson had about 25,000 residents.*

THE IRISH POTATO FAMINE

The main food of the Irish people was the potato. Between 1845–1851 the crop failed. About a million people died of hunger and another million people emigrated, mostly to the U.S. Millions more have emigrated since. Today, Ireland's population is about half the 8 million it was before 1845.

▼ *Immigration into America between 1815 and 1914 was the largest peaceful movement of people in history. It is estimated that about 35 million people entered the U.S. during that time. Thousands of Chinese landed in the west coast states until the U.S. Congress* *restricted further entry in 1882. The overwhelming majority of the immigrants came from Europe. From 1892–1924 the chief entry point to the U.S. was Ellis Island in New York Bay. Here, would-be immigrants (below) were interviewed by immigration officers.*

Society in the 1800s

The taste and the standards of the prosperous middle class set the pattern of the West in the Victorian Age (named after Queen Victoria, who ruled Great Britain from 1837 to 1901). They were highminded, for their education was dominated by Christian teaching; their life centered on the family and the home. Many men and women were employed as domestic servants in the homes of the middle and upper classes. They received free food and board and a small salary, but in return they worked up to 70 hours a week.

1837–1901	1860s	1890s
The 63-year reign of Queen Victoria	Victorian style in design reaches its peak	Reaction against Victorian style

▲ *Most of the servants of middle-class families lived on the premises in simply-furnished rooms in the attic or cellar.*

▼ *The upper middle class in Victorian times enjoyed a highly privileged lifestyle. They lived in imposing mansions set in large grounds in leafy suburbs. They did no housework. A staff of servants ranging from the lordly butler down to the lowly scullery maid attended to all their needs.*

Middle-class Victorians

Brass four poster bed

Butler serves tea in drawing room

19th-century house, Boston, Mass.

Kitchen

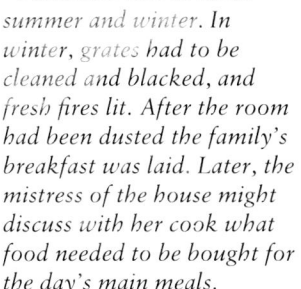

◀ *Servants rose at six in summer and winter. In winter, grates had to be cleaned and blacked, and fresh fires lit. After the room had been dusted the family's breakfast was laid. Later, the mistress of the house might discuss with her cook what food needed to be bought for the day's main meals.*

VISITING THE POOR
Many well-off people had a sense of duty toward those less fortunate than themselves. They supported societies to reform prisons and to prevent cruelty to children. They gave food and clothing to the sick and needy, and visited them in their homes.

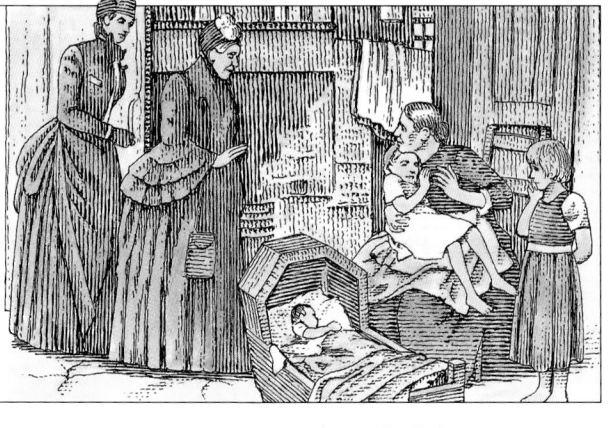

LOUIS PASTEUR
By the 1800s, the work of scientists had improved the health of people in the West. The French scientist Louis Pasteur introduced a process which kills harmful organisms in foods. He also developed the first vaccines against anthrax and rabies.

Early "boneshaker" bicycle

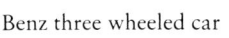
Benz three wheeled car

▼ An army of street vendors peopled city streets in the 1800s. Among them were sellers of flowers, fabric, saucepans, cage-birds, and fake medicines. Food and drink was sold—chestnuts, hot pies, ice cream, vegetables, and spices. The streets were also full of people such as chimney sweeps looking for work.

Chimney sweep

Flowergirl

Early electric light bulb

Bell's first telephone

Pie seller

▲ The 1800s was an age of invention. From America came telephones, the carpet sweeper, cash registers, the safety pin, condensed milk, slot machines, and barbed wire. British inventors contributed the electric lamp, the pneumatic tire, shorthand, and linoleum. The Germans, Daimler and Benz, developed the motor car. The first successful bicycle appeared in France.

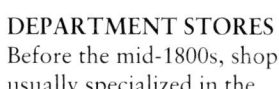
Early department store, Chicago

DEPARTMENT STORES
Before the mid-1800s, shops usually specialized in the goods they sold. The first department store (a shop carrying a wide variety of goods) opened in New York in 1848. Others soon opened across the U.S. and in western Europe.

The Colonial Age

The Industrial Revolution caused the new manufacturing powers to seach for raw materials for their factories, mineral wealth such as gold for investment, and fresh markets for their goods. European powers began to acquire many new colonies, especially in Africa, Southeast Asia, and the islands of the Pacific Ocean. From the 1870s to 1910, in the "Scramble for Africa," almost the whole of that continent was colonized by Europeans who needed its abundant supply of raw materials.

Commodore Perry in Japan, 1853

1817–1818	1860	1898
The British dominance of India begins	French begin expansion in West Africa	Spain cedes Philippines to the U.S.

▶ *In 1857, a mutiny by sepoys, the Indian soldiers in the British army in India, grew into a widespread revolt against British rule. The mutineers seized Lucknow and India's capital, Delhi. Cawnpore was captured and its British residents murdered. The British called up reinforcements and retook the captured cities, including Delhi (right). By July 1858, the rebels were defeated and the British were again in control of India.*

▲ *Japan had been isolated by its rulers from foreign contact, from the 1600s until the mid-1800s. The western powers tried, unsuccessfully, to gain admittance. In 1853, American warships under Commodore Matthew Perry anchored in Tokyo Bay. The threat of American naval power helped Perry persuade the Japanese to resume trading with the West.*

EUROPEAN COLONIES IN THE 1800s

As the 1800s ended, Britain, France, and the Netherlands occupied most of south and southeast Asia. The British ruled India, Burma, and Malaya. France had absorbed Vietnam. The United States had taken the Philippines after the Spanish-American war of 1898. The Dutch had ruled most of the East Indies ever since driving out the Portuguese in the early 1600s, but Germany occupied part of New Guinea and Britain controlled Brunei, Sarawak, and North Borneo. Of all the south Asian countries, only the kingdom of Siam was not under foreign rule. By 1914, the whole of Africa, with the exception of Ethiopia and Liberia, had either been colonized or was supervised by a European power *(see opposite page)*. Territory controlled by Britain stretched almost unbroken from Egypt to South Africa. France possessed most of West and North Africa. Germany, Italy, Portugal, and Spain held the rest of the continent.

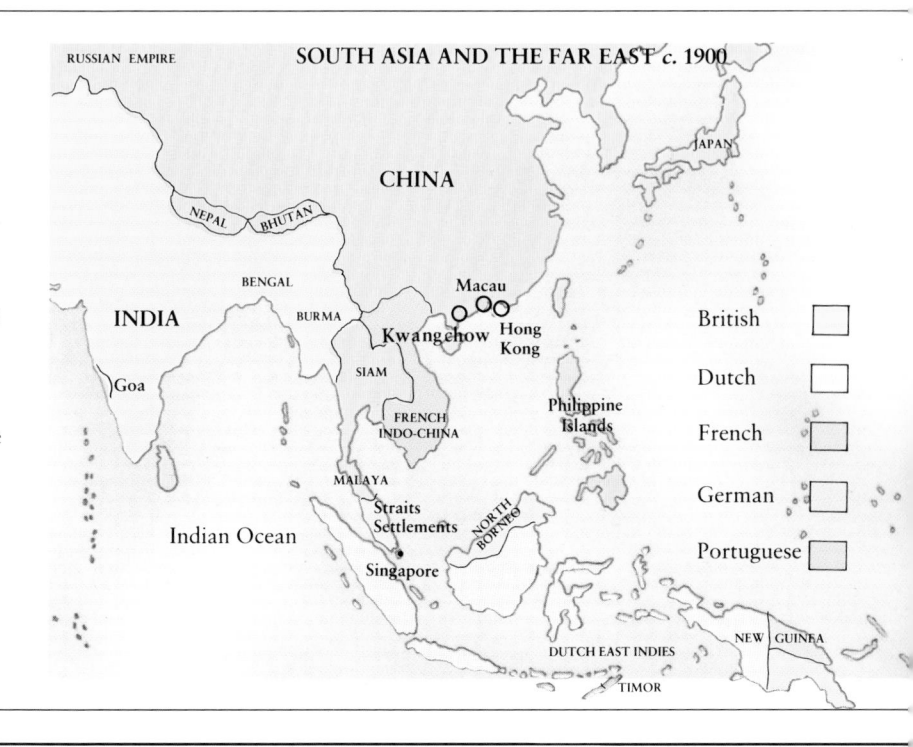

SOUTH ASIA AND THE FAR EAST c. 1900

RUSSIAN EMPIRE
CHINA
JAPAN
NEPAL
BHUTAN
BENGAL
INDIA
BURMA
Macau
Kwangchow
Hong Kong
Goa
SIAM
FRENCH INDO-CHINA
Philippine Islands
MALAYA
Straits Settlements
NORTH BORNEO
Indian Ocean
Singapore
DUTCH EAST INDIES
NEW GUINEA
TIMOR

British ☐
Dutch ☐
French ☐
German ☐
Portuguese ☐

▼ *In the scramble for colonies, France claimed Vietnam in Southeast Asia. French Catholic missionaries had been in Vietnam since the 1600s.*

After defeating the Vietnamese in a long series of wars the French made Vietnam a colony in 1887 (as French Indochina).

French soldiers fighting in North Vietnam, 1853

FURTHER FACTS

● By the end of the 1800s the British empire was the largest of all time, comprising a quarter of the globe's land surface and its inhabitants.

● French and British colonial ambitions often clashed. In 1896, the two countries resolved their rivalry in southeast Asia by agreeing to keep Siam (Thailand) as an independent buffer state between them.

● A conference in Berlin in 1884 virtually agreed that any part of Africa without a European owner could be claimed merely by arriving there and raising a national flag.

▶ *In 1839, the Chinese tried to stop the illegal importing of opium by the British. When they destroyed a large cargo of the drug, the British retaliated by landing troops and taking the city of Shanghai. Fighting only ended in 1856 with the seizure of Peking by an Anglo-French force; this opened Chinese ports to western trade.*

▼ *Throughout the 1800s, European explorers and Christian missionaries traveled deep into Africa. In 1866, the Scottish missionary and explorer, David Livingstone, disappeared while seeking the source of Nile. In a famous meeting, the American journalist H.M. Stanley met him by Lake Tanganyika.*

AFRICA IN 1914

Belgian colonies

British colonies

French colonies

German colonies

Portuguese colonies

Spanish colonies

Italian colonies

Independent African states

Part of the Ottoman empire but under British control

MOROCCO
RIO DE ORO
ALGERIA
TUNISIA
LIBYA
EGYPT
FRENCH WEST AFRICA
GAMBIA
SENEGAL
PORT. GUINEA
SIERRA LEONE
LIBERIA
GOLD COAST
DAHOMEY
NIGERIA
IVORY COAST
TOGOLAND
FRENCH EQUATORIAL AFRICA
ANGLO-EGYPTIAN SUDAN
ERITREA
ABYSSINIA
ITALIAN SOMALILAND
UGANDA
BRITISH EAST AFRICA
CABINDA
BELGIAN CONGO
GERMAN EAST AFRICA
ZANZIBAR
NYASALAND
ANGOLA
NORTHERN RHODESIA
MOZAMBIQUE
MADAGASCAR
GERMAN SOUTHWEST AFRICA
SOUTHERN RHODESIA
BECHUANALAND
UNION OF SOUTH AFRICA

THE TWO WORLD WARS

World War I

World War I (1914–1918) was the most destructive war in world history. Of the 65 million men who served in the different armies, an estimated 10 million died. Large parts of Europe were left in ruins. Some years after the war, in the late 1920s and 1930s, the world was hit by a severe economic crisis. The Great Depression began in the U.S., before spreading around the world. Thousands of businesses were ruined, and in the U.S. alone 16 million people (a third of the workforce) were out of work. The crisis forced Western governments to reshape their policies. But there was no real improvement in employment until the military aggression of Germany, Italy, and Japan created a need for more jobs in the defence and other industries in the 1940s. By then, the world had embarked on another terrible war.

August 1914	1916	November 1918
Germany invades Belgium; France, Britain declare war on Germany	Battles of Verdun and Somme create 2 million casualties	After revolt in Germany, armistice signed ending the war

▶ *Many new weapons made their appearance in World War I. Aircraft were used for the first time. Tanks ended the long stalemate of trench warfare. Poison gas added to the terrors of the battlefield. At sea, no surface vessel, not even the new great battleships, were immune to attack by submarines.*

German trench on Western front

German Fokker triplane

British MK IV tank

FURTHER FACTS

● In June 1914, a Serbian terrorist assassinated the heir to the Austrian throne in Sarajevo, Bosnia. Within six weeks Europe was at war— Germany and the Austro–Hungarian empire ranged themselves against France, Britain, and Russia.
● The sinking of American merchant ships by German submarines brought the U.S. into the war in 1917. The fresh troops, backed by the resources of the U.S., caused the final defeat of Germany.

Gas mask

UB II German submarine

British battleship HMS *Dreadnought*

WORLD WAR I
1914–1918

Central Powers

Allied Powers

Neutral

NORWAY · SWEDEN · GREAT BRITAIN · London · NETHERLANDS · Brussels · BELGIUM · LUX. · Somme · Paris · Verdun · Western front · FRANCE · SWITZ. · Atlantic Ocean · PORTUGAL · SPAIN · ITALY · Rome · ALBANIA · SERBIA · Sarajevo · GREECE · Moscow · RUSSIA · Berlin · GERMANY · Brest-Litovsk · Farthest Austro-German penetration · Vienna · AUSTRIA-HUNGARY · BULGARIA · Constantinople · Gallipoli · OTTOMAN EMPIRE

◄ *World War I changed the map of Europe. In the east, Poland, Latvia, Lithuania, and Estonia became independent states. Hungary become a separate republic from Austria. A new state, Czechoslovakia, was created in central Europe. Serbia, Croatia, and Slovenia united under a king in an attempt to solve the long-term problems of the Balkan states.*

THE TREATY OF VERSAILLES

The treaty signed in June 1919 ended the war. The British, French, and American statesmen who drew it up hoped it would make the world safe from future conflicts. It founded the League of Nations to solve future disputes between states. The League cleared up minor issues but failed to settle major problems. The Germans resented the harsh terms imposed on them and as they recovered from the war they became increasingly hostile toward the League and its members. Once more, Europe became divided into two armed camps.

▲ *Despite its casualties, World War I was fought without a single decisive battle on the Western Front. For over four years, fighting centered around two lines of trenches, stretching across western Europe. As the war dragged on, life in the dirty, waterlogged trenches became intolerable for the soldiers who lived in them.*

THE RUSSIAN REVOLUTION

By the end of 1916, the better-equipped Germany army had brought the Russian army near to defeat. In order to reduce Russia to even further chaos, the Germans smuggled the marxist revolutionary Vladimir Lenin (depicted *right* in a 1930s' painting) back into Russia from exile abroad. In November 1917, Lenin's Bolshevik (later Communist) party made an attempt to overthrow the Russian government. The troops sent to put down the uprising joined the rioting crowds. Strikes in Petrograd (St. Petersburg) grew into a full-scale revolution which saw the downfall of the monarchy and the eventual establishment of a communist dictatorship in Russia.

The Great Depression

After World War I, democratic governments often seemed too weak and indecisive to handle the problems of peacetime, especially the economic crisis of the Depression. Both Italy and Germany became dictatorships under men who promised strong leadership and simple cures for their nation's woes. After a savage civil war, Franco emerged as Spain's leader. The U.S.S.R. was governed by the tyrannical Joseph Stalin, who forced through a series of ruthless social policies in order to modernize his country.

January 1920
League of Nations'
first meeting

January 1933
Hitler becomes
German Chancellor

September 1939
German army
invades Poland

PARTITION OF IRELAND
Ireland had been dominated by Britain since the 1100s. At Easter in 1916, British troops crushed a revolt in Dublin by Irish nationalists seeking independence. In 1918, the nationalists declared Ireland an independent state, and the Anglo-Irish treaty of 1921 recognized the independence of southern Ireland as the Irish Free State. The six mainly Protestant counties of Ulster remained part of the UK.

◀ *Dublin's post office was at the center of the 1916 uprising.*

Queue of
unemployed
in 1930s

▲ *As world trade declined in the 1930s, millions were thrown out of work throughout the West. Banks collapsed, and people lost their savings. The unemployed rioted and everywhere lines for jobs lengthened. In the U.S., this human-engineered calamity was made worse by a natural disaster. In 1934 and 1935, the Midwest was stricken by severe drought. Intensive farming had exhausted the soil and, as the crops died, there was nothing to bind it together. Gales arose and blew the soil away. Thousands of farmers and their families were forced off the land, their livelihoods ruined (left).*

◄ *In Europe the sacrifices of war had been followed by economic suffering. These difficult times provided opportunities for both the German Nazi Party under Adolf Hitler, and Benito Mussolini's Italian Fascist party. Both men came to power promising national recovery. Millions of their fellow citizens believed them. Soon both leaders were also seeking territorial expansion in Europe.*

Hitler at Nazi rally

Republican poster in Spanish Civil War

◄ *In 1936, officers of the Spanish army led by General Franco, rebelled against their government. The revolt swiftly became a civil war. Foreign states got involved. The fascist (extreme right-wing) powers, Germany and Italy, sent help to the army and its right-wing supporters. Communist Russia aided the government. By 1939, most of Spain had been overrun by the rebels and their leader General Franco was appointed head of state.*

Russian tractors in 1930s

▲ *Lenin died in 1924 and Joseph Stalin succeeded him as head of the U.S.S.R. Stalin set out to strip farmers of their land in order to reorganize farming in larger state-owned units called collectives. His orders were brutally carried out by the army and secret police. Villages were burned and their people killed. Millions were forcibly transported to labor camps in Siberia.*

MASS CULTURE

The new means of communication and travel which appeared between the wars started to break down the old barriers between classes and nations. The first worldwide form of mass culture was the movies. Film actors like the comedian Charlie Chaplin became international idols. In travel, faster airplanes brought the countries of the world closer together, and mass-produced cars increased private travel. In the 1930s, radio and the first television services brought information and entertainment to millions in their own homes.

Charlie Chaplin

Early radio

Handley Page HP42 airplane, 1931

Model "T" Ford

FURTHER FACTS

- **1919:** The German Nazi party and the Italian Fascist party were both founded.
- **1924:** The American Ford motor company produced its ten millionth car.
- **1935:** British publisher Allen Lane, launched mass-market paperbacks with Penguin Books.
- **1939:** Pan American Airlines began the first regular transatlantic air service.

World War II

American *Mustang P51* fighter plane

World War II was an even more destructive war than World War I. Over 50 million people died, the great majority of them innocent civilians. It was caused by the military aggression of three countries—Italy, Germany, and Japan (the Axis Powers). At first the Axis won a string of victories. But not one of the three countries had enough resources for a long war. They were eventually defeated by the superior numbers and technology of the Allies—the British Commonwealth, France, U.S.S.R., and the United States.

German *Tiger Tank*

September 1939
Britain and France declare war on Germany

April 1945
Hitler kills himself; Germany surrenders to Allies in May

August 1945
Japan accepts Allied surrender terms

Japanese battleship *Yomoto*

German V2 rocket

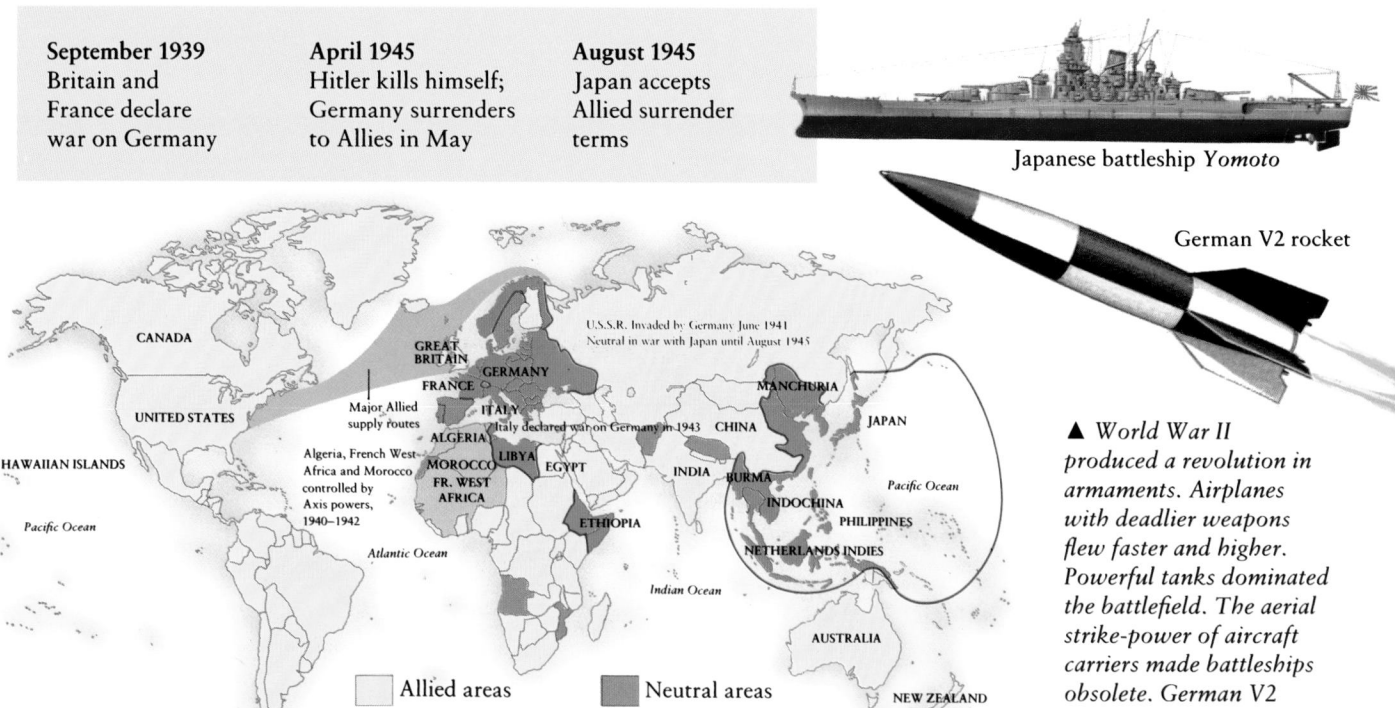

Allied areas Neutral areas

Axis occupied areas — Axis expansion

▲ World War II produced a revolution in armaments. Airplanes with deadlier weapons flew faster and higher. Powerful tanks dominated the battlefield. The aerial strike-power of aircraft carriers made battleships obsolete. German V2 rockets gave a terrifying foretaste of future wars.

▲ Both Germany and Japan made huge gains early in the war. Germany dominated the whole of continental Europe. Japan overran the western Pacific and conquered Southeast Asia and the East Indies. As the war went on, the Russians, Americans, British, and their allies regained the lost territories and forced the Axis Powers to surrender.

▶ In 1941, the Americans and the Japanese were discussing peace in the Pacific. On December 7 1941 Japanese planes made a surprise attack on ships of the U.S. fleet based at Pearl Harbor in Hawaii. Within half an hour the U.S. fleet had been crippled. The next day, the U.S. president Franklin D. Roosevelt declared war on Japan and the other Axis Powers.

THE HOLOCAUST

The most appalling aspect of the Nazi regime was the persecution and extermination of the Jews. Violent attacks on Jews in Germany began in the 1930s and were continued in all the countries the Germans occupied. Death camps were established for the sole purpose of eliminating the entire Jewish population. Altogether, nearly 6 million Jews were murdered.

▶ *Jewish families are herded by German guards onto cattle trucks for transportation to one of several European death camps.*

▶ *In August 1943, Hitler ordered his armies in Russia to capture Stalingrad. By November they had taken most of the city. Then the Russians counterattacked. Cut off, short of food, and without warm clothing in the Russian winter, the German troops surrendered. This defeat was a major turning point in the war.*

▼ *By the 1940s, bombing raids meant that civilians far from the battlefields had become directly involved in wars. In German air attacks on Britain about 70,000 people died, and about a million Germans died from the Allied bombing raids. A million Japanese civilians were killed by American bombs.*

▼ *In July 1945, America's new president, Harry Truman, gave permission to drop the first atomic bombs on Japan. The bomb that fell on Hiroshima on August 6 caused up to 130,000 deaths. Three days later a second bomb on the city of Nagasaki caused up to 750,000 deaths. The terror the bombs caused persuaded the Japanese to surrender.*

A mushroom cloud forms after the first atom bomb was dropped on Hiroshima

THE POSTWAR WORLD

The Cold War

After the war, world power became divided between two superpowers, the U.S.S.R. and the United States of America. Instead of disarming, the former wartime partners became rivals in an increasingly dangerous arms race. The result was the so-called "Cold War," in which a state of hostility existed for decades between the superpowers without actually leading to major conflict. The United Nations, set up at the end of World War II to keep the peace, was powerless to influence the conduct of its two most powerful members. China became communist under Mao Zedong, wars in Korea and Indochina followed, as the U.S. attempted to contain communist influence in Southeast Asia. Superpower rivalry in space technology and travel also led to the race to be first on the Moon, a race won by the United States in 1969.

January 1946
First meeting
of the UN
General Assembly

1961
Berlin Wall built as
a barrier between
East and West

August 1963
U.S., U.S.S.R., and Britain
sign nuclear test
ban treaty

EUROPE DURING THE COLD WAR
After World War II the wartime cooperation between the U.S.S.R. and the Western allies collapsed. An "iron curtain" of mistrust fell between them. By 1950, Europe was cut in two by a string of minefields and border posts which stretched from the Baltic in the north to the Black Sea in the south. In 1949, the Western powers formed a military alliance (North Atlantic Treaty Organization) to fight any Soviet attack.

NATO countries (also includes Canada, U.S., and Iceland)

Warsaw pact

Neutral countries

FINLAND
NORWAY
SWEDEN
IRELAND
UNITED KINGDOM
DENMARK
NETHERLANDS
BELGIUM
POLAND
E GERMANY
W GERMANY
LUX.
CZECHOSLOVAKIA
FRANCE
SWITZ.
AUSTRIA
HUNGARY
ROMANIA
YUGOSLAVIA
PORTUGAL
SPAIN
ITALY
BULGARIA
ALBANIA
GREECE
TURKEY
U.S.S.R.

Allied planes unloading supplies for Berlin, 1949

◀ In 1945, Germany and its former capital Berlin were divided into four Allied occupation zones. In 1948, the Soviets cut all land links between western Germany and the Allied sectors in Berlin. The Allies then airlifted goods into West Berlin. The Soviets allowed the flights to continue in case war broke out. In 1949, Germany split into two states, East and West Germany.

在毛澤東的勝利旗幟下前進

CHINA TURNS COMMUNIST

When the war in Asia and the Pacific ended, a struggle began between the nationalist government under Chiang Kai-shek and the communists led by Mao Zedong (left) to decide the future of China. Chiang's forces outnumbered the communists by ten to one but his regime was corrupt and his army poorly trained. His troops deserted in droves and city after city fell to the communists. In 1949, in the capital Peking (Beijing), Mao proclaimed the establishment of the People's Republic of China under communist control.

▼ *The United Nations was founded in 1945 by the wartime Allies. Its purposes are to maintain international peace and to solve problems through international cooperation. Since 1945 the UN's forces have been involved in several conflicts including Korea, the Middle East, and Yugoslavia.*

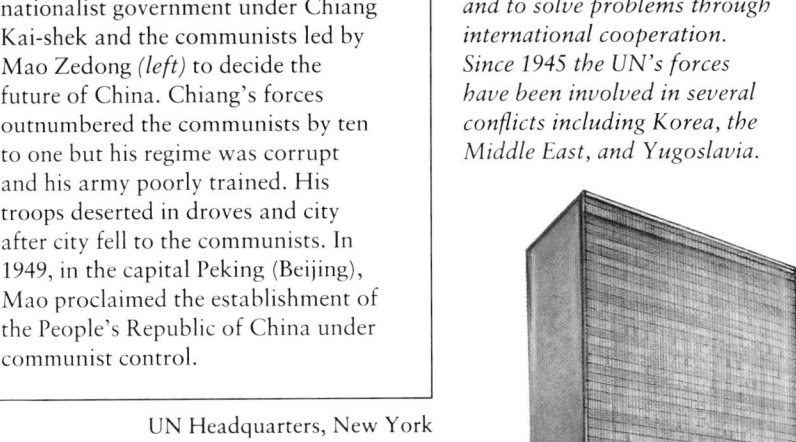

UN Headquarters, New York

◄ *In 1950, North Korea's Soviet-trained army crossed into South Korea. The United Nations condemned the invasion. For the first time, a major international, although mainly American, force gathered under the UN flag. The UN army landed in South Korea and by 1953 North Korea and its Chinese allies were forced to recognize South Korea's independence.*

FURTHER FACTS

● **1948**: Organization for European Economic Cooperation (OEEC) founded. It has since developed into the European Community (EC).

● **1949**: North Atlantic Treaty Organization formed (NATO)—a military alliance between the U.S. and her allies in western Europe.

● **1955**: U.S.S.R. and her allies sign the Warsaw Pact, an East European defence treaty.

► *Cuba was the center of a major international crisis in 1962. In 1961, a failed invasion of the island, backed by the U.S., confirmed the alliance of Cuba's marxist ruler Fidel Castro with the U.S.S.R. During 1962, Soviet nuclear missiles, capable of hitting American cities, were installed in Cuba. U.S. president John Kennedy ordered a naval blockade of Cuba. Nuclear war threatened but the Soviets withdrew their missiles while the U.S. promised not to invade Cuba.*

Missile launchers in Cuba

The World Transformed

The greatest changes of the 1900s have been caused by the dramatic advances in science and technology. New forms of transport, entertainment, household appliances, and medical advances are only a few of the areas that have improved the quality of life for most of us. In the past 50 years computers have enabled people to totally transform the world we live in. Used first in business, they are now found in almost every aspect of human life from medicine and education to home entertainment.

1950s	1960s	1980s
Elvis Presley begins pop music revolution	High point of pop art and op art	Madonna's first album "Madonna" released

▶ *In 1957, the U.S.S.R. launched the first artificial satellite to stay up in space. Soviet scientists followed this success by putting the first person into orbit in April 1961. Americans were humiliated by the U.S.S.R.'s clear lead in space technology. In May 1961, President Kennedy committed the United States to landing an astronaut on the Moon before the end of the decade. Billions of dollars were poured into a U.S. space program. On July 20, 1969, stepping from the lunar module* Eagle, *U.S. astronaut Neil Armstrong became the first human being to set foot on the Moon.*

Fourth landing of American astronauts on the Moon, 1971

▼ *Buying cooked food to be eaten on the spot is not new. Hot dogs, pizzas, and burritos have been sold for many years. But this industry has grown enormously in recent decades, with more restaurants selling food that is prepared quickly and easily.*

Eating fast food

▼ *Computers can perform millions of calculations in seconds. They help to design and manufacture many things, including cars, more quickly and cheaply and are becoming increasingly important in business, education, and the home.*

Personal computer

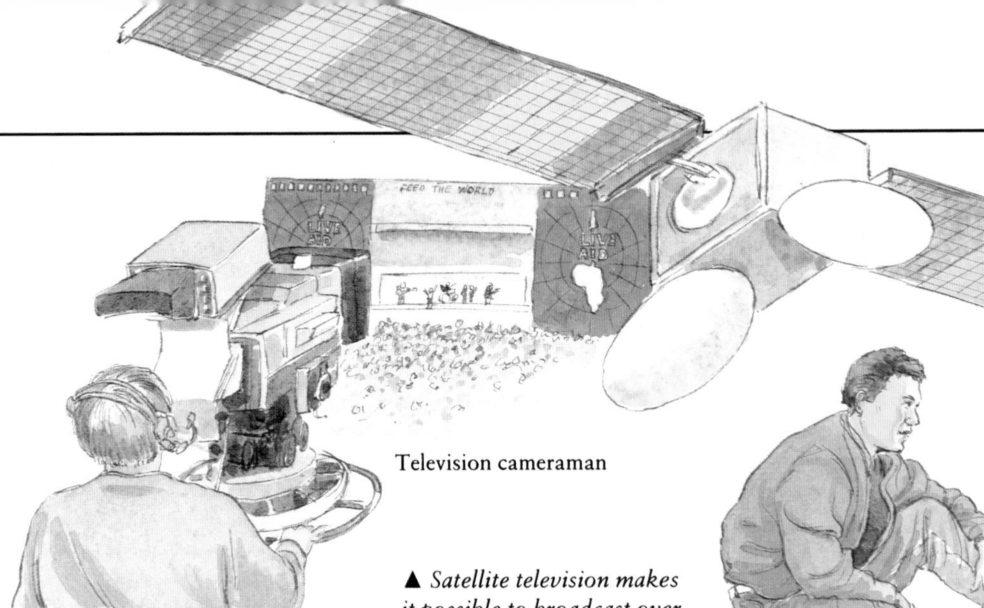

Communications satellite

Television cameraman

▲ *Satellite television makes it possible to broadcast over vast distances and to several countries at the same time. The first such television broadcast took place in July 1964, when the American satellite Telstar relayed the Olympic Games around the world from Tokyo.*

▶ *Increased pollution is a price we pay for living in the late 1900s. Engine fumes pouring from thousands of vehicles stuck in city traffic jams not only poison human lungs but eat away the fabric of the buildings in which we work and live.*

Traffic jam in American city

FURTHER FACTS

- **1958**: Opening of Guggenheim Museum, New York, designed by Frank Lloyd Wright.
- **1958**: Niemeyer designs the president's palace in Brasília.
- **1985**: Pop singer Bob Geldof organizes "Live Aid," the famous global pop concert, to help raise money for world famine.

TWENTIETH CENTURY CULTURE

In the late 1900s, art and music have developed into popular forms of culture, particularly for young people. In the '50s Elvis Presley became the first rock star with a massive following; later, the Beatles enjoyed unprecedented success. In the 1990s, stars such as Madonna are made world famous with promotion. U.S. artist Roy Lichtenstein used comic strips, advertisements, and other common images and made them subjects of art. The American author, Toni Morrison, writes prize-winning books that explore the subject of Black American relationships. New materials and technologies enable architects to design elegant structures of glass and metals. Englishman Henry Moore's sculptures seem to grow naturally from the landscape around them.

Blam by Roy Lichtenstein

Madonna, American entertainer

Reclining Figure by Henry Moore

Toni Morrison, American Pulitzer Prize winning writer

Itamaraty Palace, Brasilia

Retreat from Empire

The old European empires were speedily dismantled in the years following World War II. The effort of fighting the war had weakened the European powers and they became incapable of resisting the various nationalist movements that had grown up in their overseas possessions. India's independence in 1947 began the breakup of the British empire. Between 1950 and 1980 more than 45 former African colonies became independent countries, as well as the majority of Asian and Middle Eastern colonies.

■ Countries that have become independent since 1950

▲ Between 1950 and 1980 most colonies became independent states. The majority were to be found in Africa, south of the Sahara.

1947
India, divided into India and Pakistan, becomes independent

1965–1980
Ruling white minority in Rhodesia (now Zimbabwe) refuses Black majority rule

1954–1975
Wars in Vietnam, involving western powers of France and U.S.

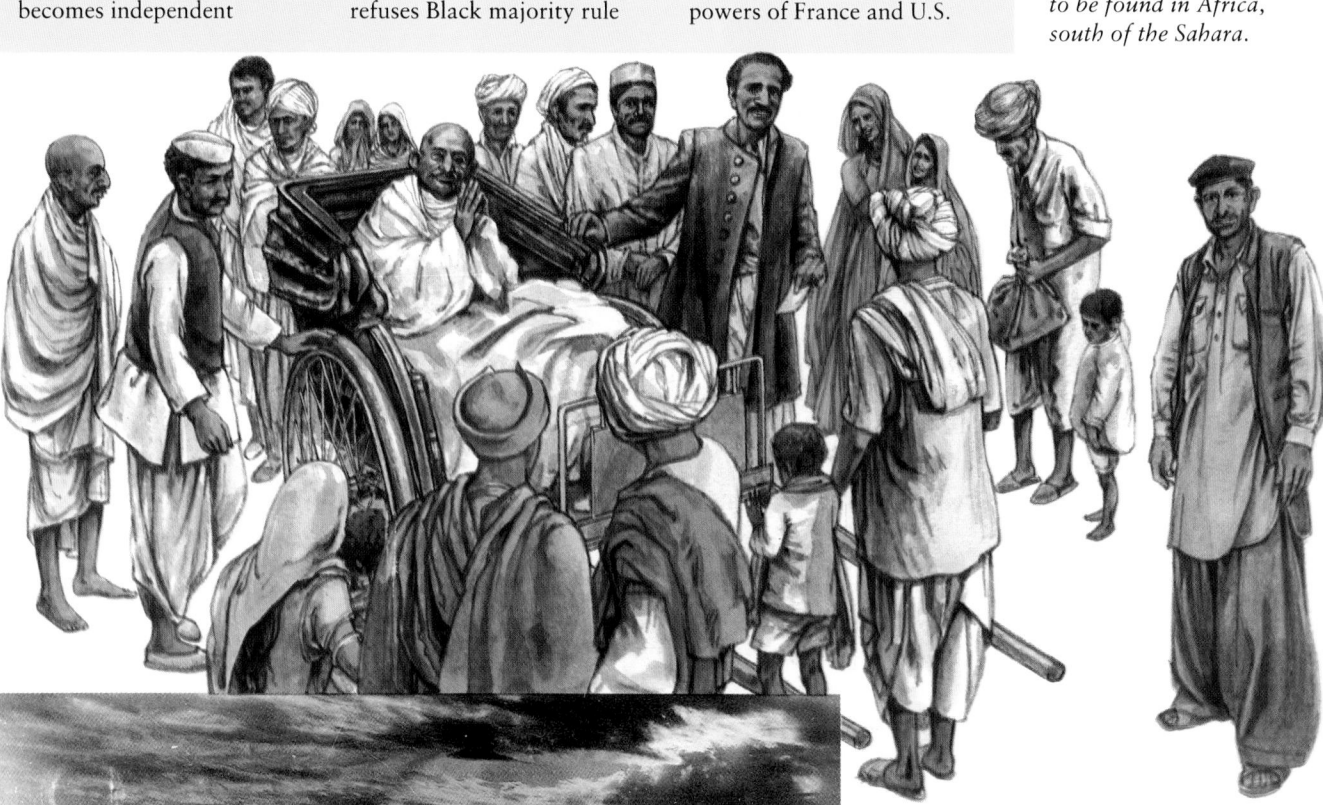

▲ Mohandas Gandhi known as "Mahatma" (Great Soul) led India to independence from the British. He organized passive resistance to British rule on a mass scale and was imprisoned several times. India won independence in 1947, but Gandhi was assassinated in 1948 by a Hindu fanatic.

◄ Algeria had been French since 1848 and many French colonists had settled there. The refusal of the settlers to grant equal rights to the native Muslim population caused increasing unrest. In 1954, a major revolt led by the Front de Libération Nationale (FLN) resulted in seven years of savage fighting. Algeria became an independent republic in July 1962.

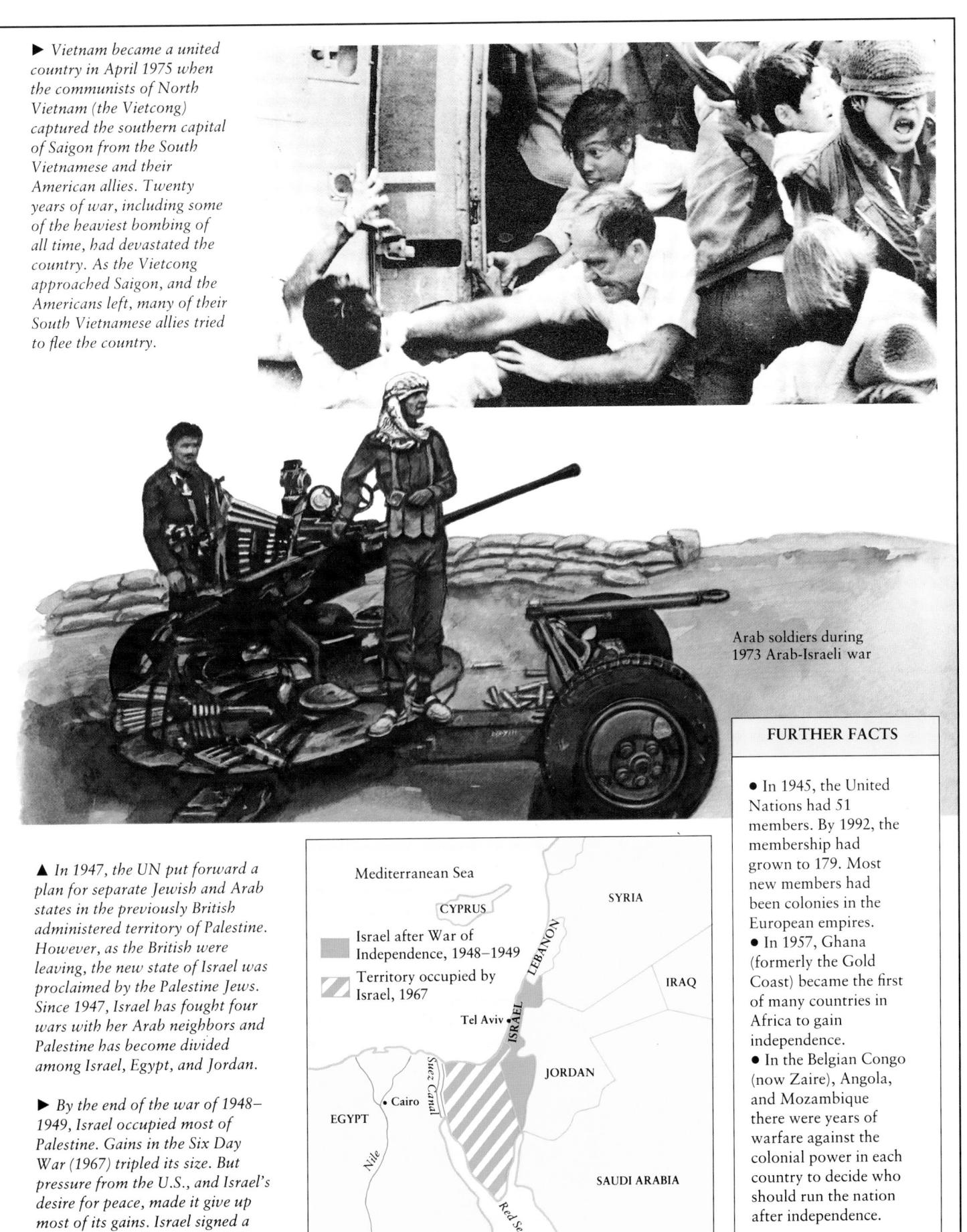

▶ *Vietnam became a united country in April 1975 when the communists of North Vietnam (the Vietcong) captured the southern capital of Saigon from the South Vietnamese and their American allies. Twenty years of war, including some of the heaviest bombing of all time, had devastated the country. As the Vietcong approached Saigon, and the Americans left, many of their South Vietnamese allies tried to flee the country.*

Arab soldiers during 1973 Arab-Israeli war

▲ *In 1947, the UN put forward a plan for separate Jewish and Arab states in the previously British administered territory of Palestine. However, as the British were leaving, the new state of Israel was proclaimed by the Palestine Jews. Since 1947, Israel has fought four wars with her Arab neighbors and Palestine has become divided among Israel, Egypt, and Jordan.*

▶ *By the end of the war of 1948– 1949, Israel occupied most of Palestine. Gains in the Six Day War (1967) tripled its size. But pressure from the U.S., and Israel's desire for peace, made it give up most of its gains. Israel signed a peace treaty with Egypt in 1979.*

Mediterranean Sea

CYPRUS

SYRIA

LEBANON

IRAQ

Israel after War of Independence, 1948–1949

Territory occupied by Israel, 1967

Tel Aviv

ISRAEL

JORDAN

Suez Canal

Cairo

EGYPT

Nile

SAUDI ARABIA

Red Sea

FURTHER FACTS

● In 1945, the United Nations had 51 members. By 1992, the membership had grown to 179. Most new members had been colonies in the European empires.

● In 1957, Ghana (formerly the Gold Coast) became the first of many countries in Africa to gain independence.

● In the Belgian Congo (now Zaire), Angola, and Mozambique there were years of warfare against the colonial power in each country to decide who should run the nation after independence.

The New World Order

In the early 1990s, the Cold War, which once divided the world into two armed camps, was replaced by conflict between states that had been part of the Soviet empire. Technology, which contines to make rapid advances, usually means a more agreeable life for those who can afford it. Yet pollution of land, sea, and air seems to be the penalty for the prosperity of the world's richer nations. Meanwhile, population growth, wars, and climatic change have brought severe famine to millions in Africa and Asia.

1960 Sharpeville, South Africa: troops kill 67 black demonstrators	**1986** Chernobyl, U.S.S.R.: nuclear disaster causes international pollution	**1992** U.S.S.R. splits into 15 independent republics

THE FALL OF COMMUNISM

After 1945, the Soviet Union imposed communism on the countries of eastern Europe that had fallen under its control. Any uprisings against the U.S.S.R. were ruthlessly crushed. But nationalism in eastern Europe continued. In 1985, a new leader, Mikhail Gorbachev, came to power in the U.S.S.R. Gorbachev was committed to reform. He allowed more political freedom within Russia and its subject states. Popular democratic movements sprang up in eastern Europe and led to the overthrow of their communist governments. In 1989, the most hated symbol of communist repression, the wall that divided East and West Berlin, was torn down *(below)*. By 1990, communism in Europe had collapsed.

▼ *Famine, caused by wars and climatic change, means that many millions of people in the world's poorer nations are kept alive only by foreign imported aid of food, medicine, and clothing. In Asia, Bangladesh has suffered from catastrophic flooding, while several African countries south of the Sahara Desert are turning into dry, barren wastelands, rife with starvation and disease.*

▼ *Improved farming methods, plants that give higher yields, scientific animal breeding, and irrigation schemes have greatly increased the production of food in some developing countries.*

WORLD TRADE ASSOCIATIONS SET UP SINCE 1945

- EFTA
- EC
- COMECON
- ASEAN
- OECD
- LAIA
- CACM
- OPEC

▲ *Associations between groups of countries have grown up in many parts of the world. Their objectives vary. Some are merely agreements to cooperate in economic and social matters. The aim of the European Community is eventually to form complete political union between the nations concerned.*

THE END OF APARTHEID

The apartheid laws passed in 1948 in South Africa separated the population according to race and color. White people became a privileged ruling class while non-whites were deprived of all civil rights. After 30 years of agitation in South Africa and worldwide condemnation, the apartheid laws began to be dismantled. The respected black leader Nelson Mandela was released after 26 years in prison. In 1991, the apartheid laws were repealed by the government.

Nelson Mandela

FURTHER FACTS

- The first nuclear reactor for generating electricity opened at Obninsk, the U.S.S.R. in 1954. In 1956, Britain started up the world's first large-scale nuclear power plant, at Calder Hall.
- The General Agreement on Tariffs and Trade (GATT) is an agency set up by the UN. Its purpose is to reduce tariffs and to remove barriers to trade worldwide.

GATT was established in 1958.
- The dismantling of the Berlin Wall was the most dramatic event of the end of the Cold War. On November 9 1989 East German guards were told to let people pass freely through the checkpoints. The wall, which had stood since 1961, was pickaxed and bulldozed down.

Cleaning up coast after oil slick disaster

▶ *When a fully-laden oil tanker is wrecked, marine and shore life may be wiped out. Local fishing is destroyed and pollution can remain for many years over a wide area. The risk of such a disaster is considerable, for at any given moment the world's combined tanker fleets are transporting a billion tons of crude oil across the high seas. The sinking of the tanker* Braer *off one of the Shetland Isles in northern Scotland in January 1993 has been a catastrophe both for the people of the islands, and for the sea birds and animals that live there.*

PEOPLE IN WORLD HISTORY

Words in **bold** indicate an entry elsewhere in People in World History and Key Dates in World History.

Akbar the Great (1542–1605): Mogul emperor of India (1556–1605). Conquered most of India. Supported writers and artists and allowed freedom of worship.

Alexander the Great (356–323 B.C.): King of Macedon and greatest soldier of ancient times. Conquests stretched from Egypt to India; introduced Greek ideas to other lands.

Augustus (63 B.C.–A.D. 14): First emperor of Rome (27 B.C.–A.D. 14). During his reign Rome was peaceful and prosperous.

Babar (1483–1530): First Mogul emperor. Descendant of **Tamerlane**; invaded northern India; began 200 years of Mogul rule.

Bach, Johann Sebastian (1685–1750): German composer. Wrote concertos, sacred cantatas, keyboard works, *St. Matthew Passion*, and *B Minor Mass*.

Beethoven, Ludwig van (1770–1827): German composer. Wrote sonatas, symphonies, chamber music, concertos, and opera *Fidelio*, considered to be among finest written.

Bismarck, Otto von (1815–1898): German statesman, known as "the Iron Chancellor." Was instrumental in uniting Germany under Prussian crown in 1871.

Bolívar, Simón (1783–1830): South American revolutionary leader. Led resistance which freed several South American countries from Spanish rule in early 1800s.

Buddha (Siddhartha Gautama) (c. 563–c.480 B.C.): Founder of Buddhism. Son of a wealthy Indian ruler. Left a life of luxury to become a religious leader.

Castro, Fidel (1926–): Cuban marxist and revolutionary. President of Cuba (1959–). Supported revolutions in Africa and Latin America.

Catherine II ("the Great") (1729–1796): Russian empress. German princess, who married future Russian tsar Peter III. Became empress after his murder in 1762. During her reign Russia gained the Crimea and most of Poland.

Charlemagne (c. 742–814): King of the Franks and emperor of the West. Empire included Italy, France, and most of Germany and Spain. Defended western Europe against Moors, Saxons, and Norsemen.

Charles I (1600–1649): King of England (1625–1648). After defeat in Civil War (1642–1648) was tried by a parliamentary court and publicly executed.

Chiang Kai-shek (1887–1975): General and leader of Chinese Nationalist party. President of separate Chinese state of Taiwan (1950).

Churchill, Sir Winston (1874–1965): British statesman, soldier and author. Prime minister (1940–1945 and 1951–1955). Helped maintain British resistance to Nazi Germany. Won Nobel Prize for Literature (1953).

Columbus, Christopher (1451–1506): Italian explorer. "Discovered" New World (actually Caribbean islands) by accident while seeking route to Asia.

Constantine I ("the Great") (c. 274–337): First Christian Roman emperor. Divided Roman empire into East and West. Founded Constantinople as capital of the Eastern empire.

Cook, James (1728–1779): English explorer and navigator. Explored coasts of Australia and New Zealand.

Cortés, Hernán (1485–1547): Spanish conquistador. Conquered Aztec empire and added Mexico to the Spanish empire.

Cromwell, Oliver (1599–1658): English soldier and statesman. General in parliamentary army in English Civil War. Lord Protector (1653–1658).

Eisenhower, Dwight D. (1890–1969): General and 34th president of the U.S. (1953–1961). Supreme commander of Allied invasion of Europe in World War II (1944).

Elizabeth I (1533–1603): Queen of England (1558–1603). Daughter of **Henry VIII**; reign saw England become important European power; also a golden age of English drama.

Franco, Francisco (1892–1975): Spanish general and statesman. Leader of fascist Falange party; led nationalist rebels to victory in Spanish Civil War (1936–1939). *Caudillo* (ruler) of Spain (1939–1975).

Frederick II ("the Great") (1712–1786): King of Prussia (1740–1786). Made Prussia a leading power in Europe. Patron of writers, philosophers, and musicians.

Gama, Vasco da (c. 1469–1524): Portuguese navigator and explorer. Led first European expedition to reach India around the Cape of Good Hope (1497–1499).

Gandhi, Mohandas (1869–1948): Indian reformer and political leader, called "Mahatma" (Great Soul). Led movement for Indian independence and sought to end caste system.

Garibaldi, Giuseppe (1807–1882): Italian freedom fighter and soldier. Leader in struggle (Risorgimento) that united Italy in 1860s.

Genghis Khan (c.1167–1227): Mongol leader. Conquered an empire stretching from China to Black Sea.

Gorbachev, Mikhail (1931–): President of U.S.S.R. (1988–1991). Introduced policies of *glasnost* (openness) and *perestroika* (restructuring). Awarded Nobel Peace Prize (1990).

Hadrian (76–138): Roman emperor (117–138). Ordered building of Hadrian's Wall in northern England as a frontier against invading tribes.

Henry VIII (1491–1547): King of England (1509–1547). Removed English Church from papal control and became supreme head of Church of England. Ordered monasteries to close down and seized their wealth. Married six times.

Hitler, Adolf (1889–1945): German dictator. Founder of National Socialism (Nazi party). German chancellor (1933). Led Germany into war in 1939 by invading Poland. Committed suicide at end of war.

Ho Chi Minh (1890–1969): Vietnamese nationalist leader. Fought French colonial regime (1946–1954). First president of North Vietnam (1954–1969). Led struggle against U.S.-supported South Vietnam.

Jesus Christ (c.4 B.C.–c.A.D. 30): Central figure of Christian religion. A Jew, born in Palestine. After three-year preaching mission, tried and crucified as a political agitator.

Joan of Arc (c.1412–1431): National heroine of France. Heard "voices" telling her to free France from English invaders. After early successes, was captured by the English and burned at the stake as a witch.

Kennedy, John F. (1917–1963): 35th U.S. president (1961–1963). Two major foreign policy crises during presidency were invasion of Cuba (1961) and Cuban Missile Crisis (1962). Assassinated in Dallas, Texas.

Lenin, Vladimir (1870–1924): Russian revolutionary. Founder of Bolshevik (later Communist) party. Led Russian Revolution (1917). Premier and virtual dictator of new communist state.

Leonardo da Vinci (1452–1519): Italian artist and scientist. Considered to be supreme example of Renaissance genius. Paintings include the *Last Supper* fresco and the *Mona Lisa*.

Lincoln, Abraham (1809–1865): 16th U.S. president (1861–1865). Opposed extension of slavery. Led Northern states in American Civil War (1861–1865). Assassinated 1865.

Louis XIV (1638–1715): King of France (164–1715). Known as "the Sun King." All-powerful, absolute monarch. Persecutor of French Protestants (Huguenots). Patron of arts; built palace at Versailles.

Luther, Martin (1483–1546): German religious leader. Prime mover in Protestant Reformation.

Magellan, Ferdinand (*c*.1480–1521): Portuguese navigator. Commanded first expedition to sail around the world (1519–1522). Was killed in Philippines on the return journey.

Mandela, Nelson (1918–): Leader of African National Congress in South Africa. Imprisoned 1962–1989. Has since campaigned for democratic, multiracial society.

Mao Zedong or Mao Tse-tung (1893–1976): Chinese Marxist revolutionary leader. Overthrew nationalist government after 20-year struggle. First chairman of Peoples' Republic of China (1949–1976).

Marx, Karl (1818–1863): German philosopher and economist. Co-author (with Friedrich Engels) of *Communist Manifesto* (1848). Exiled to England, wrote *Das Kapital*, key publication of communist philosophy.

Mozart, Wolfgang Amadeus 1756–1791): Austrian composer. Works include more than 40 symphonies, nearly 30 piano concertos, and several operas (*Don Giovanni, The Marriage of Figaro*).

Muhammad (*c*.570–632): Prophet and founder of Islamic faith. His sayings are collected in the Koran. Islam counts its dates from his flight to Yathrib (now Medina) after a plot to murder him (622).

Mussolini, Benito (1883–1945): Leader (*Il Duce*) of Italian fascism. Seized power (1922); allied with Hitler in World War II. Replaced after invasion of Italy by Allies (1943); executed by Italian partisans.

Napoleon I (**Bonaparte**) (1769–1821): Emperor of France (1804–1814).

Rose to power during French Revolution. After series of military victories, established French empire. Downfall began with invasion of Russia (1812). Final defeat at Waterloo (1815); exiled to St Helena.

Nelson, Horatio (1758–1805): English admiral. Victories during Napoleonic wars kept England safe from invasion; died commanding fleet at Trafalgar (1805).

Peter I ("the Great") (1672–1725): Tsar of Russia (1682–1725). Visited western Europe to study European industrial techniques. Reformed Russian armed forces, government, alphabet, and calendar. Built city of St. Petersburg as capital.

Philip II (1527–1598): King of Spain (1556–1598), husband of Mary, Catholic queen of England (1554-1558). Strongly anti-Protestant; attempted invasion of England during reign of **Elizabeth I**, Mary's sister, but Armada was defeated (1588).

Pizarro, Francisco (*c*.1478–1541): Spanish conquistador. Conquered Inca empire in Peru with less than 200 men (1532) and killed their emperor, Atahualpa.

Polo, Marco (*c*.1254–*c*.1324): Venetian traveller. Lived at court of Kublai Khan in China. Account of his travels (1271–1295) gave Europeans their first glimpse of life in Asia.

Rembrandt (**Harmenszoon van Rijn**) (1606–1669): Dutch painter. Greatest achievements are portraits which show deep insight into human character. Works include *The Night Watch*, *The Anatomy Lesson of Dr. Tulp*, and self-portraits.

Robespierre, Maximilien (1758–1794): French revolutionary. Lawyer who became leader of Jacobins, most extreme party in French Revolution. Removed rivals during Reign of Terror, but was later arrested and guillotined.

Roosevelt, Franklin Delano (1882–1945): 32nd president of the U.S. (1933–1945) for a record four terms. His "New Deal" program rescued America from Great Depression of 1930s. Coordinated Allied war effort after American entry in World War II.

Rubens, Peter Paul (1577–1640): Flemish painter, considered a master of the baroque style. Painted portraits, landscapes, religious, and historical subjects.

Saladin (1137–1193): Sultan of Egypt and Muslim warrior. Recaptured Jerusalem and most of Palestine from the Crusaders. Renowned for his military prowess, religious tolerance and justice to his enemies.

Shakespeare, William (1564–1616): English dramatist and poet. Wrote tragedies (*Hamlet*), histories (*Richard III*), and comedies (*Twelfth Night*), generally regarded as among finest plays in the English language.

Stalin, Joseph (1879–1953): Russian communist dictator. Sole ruler of U.S.S.R. from 1927. Led Russia during World War II. Ruthlessly wiped out any opposition to his rule.

Tamerlane or **Timur** (*c*. 1336–1404): Mongol conqueror and ruler of Turkistan. Seized large parts of central Asia and Near East.

Truman, Harry S. (1884–1972): 33rd president of the U.S. (1945–1953). Took decision to drop atomic bomb on Japan (1945). Established NATO (1949). Sent U.S. troops to join UN forces resisting communist invasion of South Korea (1950).

Victoria (1819–1901): Queen of United Kingdom (1837–1901) and empress of India (from 1876). Reigned over British empire at height of its power; gave her name to the period.

Washington, George (1732–1799): General and 1st president of the U.S. (1789–1797). Commander-in-chief of Continental Army which fought British during American Revolution (1775–1783).

Wilberforce, William (1759–1833): British statesman and reformer. As Member of Parliament campaigned for abolition of slavery. His Abolition Bill became law in 1807.

Wilhelm II (1859–1941): King of Prussia and emperor of Germany (1888–1918). Ruled personally after dismissing his chancellor **Bismarck** (1890). Abdicated after Germany lost World War I.

William I, "the Conqueror" (*c*.1027–1087): First Norman king of England (1066–1087). Defeated Saxons under Harold at Hastings (1066). Ordered survey of England which became the Domesday Book.

Wilson, Thomas Woodrow (1856–1924): 28th president of the U.S. (1913–1921). Took America into World War I (1917). After the war, championed League of Nations as means of keeping world peace.

KEY DATES IN WORLD HISTORY

B.C.

*c.*5 million–1 million: *Homo habilis,* early ancestors of modern humans live in tropical Africa.

*c.*1.5 million: *Homo erectus* learn to make better tools than *Homo habilis.* Move into parts of Europe and Asia.

*c.*9000–8000: First farmers, in the Middle East.

*c.*9000: Tribes of hunters cross from Asia into North America.

*c.*8500: Jericho founded, world's first walled town.

*c.*7000: Pottery produced in Iran.

*c.*5500: Farming begins in Egypt.

*c.*4000–3500: Plow, wheel, and sail in use in Mesopotamia and Egypt.

*c.*3500: Mesopotamia: first writing appears in Sumer.

*c.*3000: First evidence of pottery in America.

*c.*2551: Egyptian pharaoh Khufu (or Cheops) builds pyramid at Giza.

*c.*2500–*c.*1628: Minoan civilization in Crete.

*c.*2000: Rise of Babylon.

*c.*2000–1000: Beginnings of Mayan culture in Central America.

*c.*1814–1754: First Assyrian empire.

*c.*1500–600: Hindu religion develops in India.

*c.*1300: Phoenicians develop alphabet to replace picture writing.

*c.*1200: Beginning of Jewish religion.

776: First Olympic Games in Greece.

753: Legendary founding of Rome.

550: Persian empire founded by Cyrus II; Persia conquers Assyria.

530: Accurate calendar in use in Babylonia.

*c.*500–27: Roman republic.

*c.*480: Death of the **Buddha** (Siddhartha Gautama).

480: Battle of Salamis: Persian invasion of Greece defeated.

*c.*479: Death of Confucius; his teachings became basis of Confucianism.

479–338: Years of Greek civilization's greatest achievements.

336–323: Reign of **Alexander the Great,** king of Macedon.

146: Carthage becomes Roman province of North Africa.

*c.*100: Chinese merchant ships begin trade with India.

54: Roman general Julius Caesar invades Britain.

49: Caesar conquers Gaul (France).

30: Egypt falls to Rome after defeat of Queen Cleopatra at Actium.

27: **Augustus** becomes first Roman emperor—start of Roman empire.

A.D.

25–222: Han dynasty in China begins great age of Chinese culture.

*c.*30: **Jesus Christ** crucified.

79: Volcano Vesuvius erupts and destroys Pompeii and other towns.

122–127: **Hadrian**'s Wall built as northern frontier of Roman Britain.

135: Palestine becomes Roman province of Judaea.

257: Goths invade Roman empire.

*c.*300: Yamato government established in Japan; Japanese clans practice Shinto religion.

313: **Constantine** ends persecution of Christians in Roman empire.

330: **Constantine** founds Constantinople on site of Byzantium.

391: Emperor Theodosius makes Christianity state religion.

410: Alaric the Goth captures Rome.

433: Attila becomes leader of the Huns.

470: Huns retreat from Europe.

476: End of Western Roman empire.

527–565: Justinian the Great emperor of Eastern Roman (Byzantine) empire.

529: St. Benedict founds first Christian monastery, at Monte Cassino, Italy.

*c.*570–*c.*632: Life of **Muhammad,** founder of Islam.

*c.*600: High point of Mayan civilization.

624: Buddhism becomes official religion in China.

*c.*700–1200: Kingdom of Ghana, first West African trading empire.

711: Arabs conquer most of Spain.

732: Battle of Poitiers: Charles Martel checks Arab advance into Europe.

742–814: Life of **Charlemagne,** king of Franks; first Holy Roman emperor.

750: Moors found city of Granada.

*c.*793: First Viking raids in northern Europe.

900: Anasazi begin to build pueblos in southwestern North America.

1000: Viking Leif Ericson lands in North America.

1066: **William of Normandy** invades England; becomes William I.

1071: Muslim Turks stop Christian pilgrimages to Jerusalem.

1086: **William I** orders survey of England (the Domesday Book).

1095: Pope Urban urges Christians to undertake a Crusade to free Holy Land from Muslim rule.

1096: First Crusade begins.

1097: Crusaders capture Jerusalem. Foundation of the Order of Knights Hospitalers.

*c.*1100: Growth of Ife kingdom in Nigeria.

1147–1148: Second Crusade: Crusaders fail to take Damascus.

1187: Saracen leader **Saladin** captures Jerusalem from Christians.

1189–1192: Third Crusade: Crusaders capture Jaffa. Richard I of England signs peace with Saladin.

*c.*1200–1300: Early Inca period in Peru.

1202–1204: Fourth Crusade.

1211: **Genghis Khan** leads Mongols to invade northern China.

1212: Children's Crusade.

1215: English barons force King John to sign Magna Carta, basis of English constitutional practice.

1218: Mongols under **Genghis Khan** overrun Persia.

1234: Mongols overthrow Chin empire in China.

1237: Mongols capture Moscow.

*c.*1250: Berbers establish several states in North Africa.

1260: Kublai Khan becomes ruler of the Mongol Empire.

1264: Kublai Khan founds Yuan dynasty in China.

1275–1292: **Marco Polo** in the service of Kublai Khan in China.

1291: Muslims capture Acre; end of Christian rule in Palestine.

1293: First Christian missionaries in China.

*c.*1300: Rise of Aztecs in Mexico.

*c.*1300: Emergence of Benin empire in Nigeria, West Africa.

1337–1453: Edward III of England claims French throne; Hundred Years' War between England and France.

1347–1351: Black Death comes to Europe from Asia. Millions die.

1352: Ibn Battuta, Berber scholar, recounts visit to Mali in Africa.

1364: Aztecs begin building their capital Tenochtitlán.

1368–1644: Ming dynasty in China; period of stability and prosperity.

1401: **Tamerlane,** ruler of Turkistan, conquers Damascus and Baghdad.

1415: English under King Henry V defeat French at battle of Agincourt.

1429: French led by **Joan of Arc** defeat English at Orléans. Charles VII crowned king of France at Rheims.

1431: **Joan of Arc** burned by English.

1445: German Johannes Gutenberg publishes *Gutenberg Bible,* first printed book in Europe.

1453: English lose all conquests in France except Calais. Ottoman Turks capture Constantinople; the end of Byzantine empire.

1474: William Caxton prints the first

book in English.

1462–1492: Rule of Lorenzo de Medici in city of Florence; patron of artists such as Michelangelo.

1480: Ivan III, grand prince of Muscovy, frees Russia from Mongols.

1487: Portuguese Bartolomeu Dias first European to round Cape of Good Hope, southern Africa.

1492: Christian Spaniards capture Granada, last stronghold of Moors in Spain. **Columbus** crosses Atlantic and reaches Caribbean islands.

1493: Pope divides New World between Spain and Portugal.

1493–1521: Reign of Huayna Capac, greatest Inca conqueror; founds a capital at Quito, Peru.

1497: Italian John Cabot sails from Bristol, England and reaches Newfoundland in North America.

1498: Vasco da Gama makes first European sea voyage to India.

*c.***1500:** Aztec empire at greatest extent.

1507: The New World named America after Italian navigator Amerigo Vespucci.

1510: Spaniards first import Africans as slaves to work in their American colonies.

1516: Coffee first imported into Europe.

1517: Martin Luther challenges teachings of Catholic Church. Protestant Reformation begins.

1519–1521: Spanish conquistador **Hernán Cortés** conquers Aztec empire in Mexico.

1520–1566: Reign of Suleiman the Magnificent; great age of Ottoman empire.

1526: Babar wins battle of Panipat in India and founds Mogul dynasty.

1531: The Inquisition established in Portugal. Copernicus, Polish astronomer, circulates his theory that the planets move around Sun, not Earth (the Church's teaching).

1532–1534: Francisco Pizarro conquers Inca empire in Peru.

1533–1584: Reign of Ivan IV ("the Terrible"), first tsar of Russia.

1534: English king **Henry VIII** denies authority of the Pope and breaks with Roman Catholic Church. French expedition led by Jacques Cartier reaches Labrador, Canada.

1541: Frenchman John Calvin founds Protestant movement in Geneva.

1545: Council of Trent begins Counter Reformation.

1556–1605: Reign of **Akbar**, greatest of Mogul rulers in India.

1558–1603: Reign of **Elizabeth I** of England; England stays Protestant and becomes major European power.

1562: English start shipping slaves from West Africa to Caribbean.

1571: Turks defeated by alliance of European Christian powers at sea battle of Lepanto. Turkish power in the Mediterranean checked.

1572: Massacre of 20,000 French Protestants on St. Bartholomew's Day.

1588: English defeat Spanish Armada.

1598: Edict of Nantes gives French Protestants equal rights with Catholics; ends French Wars of Religion.

1600: British East India Company founded. Tokugawa Ieyasu becomes shogun (ruler) of Japan. His descendants rule Japan for 250 years.

1602: Dutch East India Company founded.

1607: Colony of Jamestown, Virginia founded. The first permanent English settlement in North America.

1608: French traders found Quebec in Canada.

1618–1648: Thirty Years' War between Catholic and Protestant European powers.

1620: Pilgrim Fathers sail from Plymouth, England, in *Mayflower* to Massachusetts in North America.

1637: Japan begins a period of isolation from the rest of the world.

1642–1648: English Civil War.

1643–1715: Reign of **Louis XIV**; France becomes chief European power.

1644: Ming dynasty overthrown; Manchu dynasty founded in China.

1645: Dutchman Abel Tasman first European to reach Tasmania and New Zealand.

1649 King **Charles I** executed; England becomes republic until 1660.

1652: Dutch found colony at Cape of Good Hope (Cape Town).

1658–1707: Rule of Aurangzeb, last of great Mogul emperors.

1663–1699: Ottoman Turks invade central Europe.

1664: English capture New Amsterdam from Dutch. They re-name it New York.

1665: English scientist Isaac Newton discovers gravity.

1670: Hudson's Bay Company founded in England to acquire territory in Canada.

1682–1725: Reign of **Peter the Great** of Russia.

1697–1712: Dominance of Ashanti

empire in West Africa.

1700–1720: Great Northern War between Russia and Sweden.

1701–1714: War of the Spanish Succession; general European war fought over control of Spanish empire after death of Charles II of Spain.

1707: Union of England and Scotland. India: death of Aurangzeb begins decline of Mogul empire.

1733: Founding of Georgia, last of Thirteen Colonies in New England.

*c.***1750s–1850s:** Many new advances in science and technology in Europe sees start of Industrial Revolution.

1756: The Black Hole of Calcutta— British civilians imprisoned by ruler of Bengal die in tiny prison.

1756–1763: Seven Years' War caused by rivalry of Austria and Prussia in Europe, and France and Britain in North America.

1757: British defeat combined French and Indian army at Plassey. Beginning of British supremacy in India.

1757–1843: China limits foreign trade to city of Canton.

1762–1796: Reign of **Catherine the Great** of Russia.

1768–1771: During round-the-world trip English navigator and explorer **James Cook** reaches Australia and New Zealand.

1775–1783: American Revolution.

1776: American Declaration of Independence.

1782: Scot James Watt invents rotary steam engine.

1788: Britain sends first convicts to Australia; Sydney is first permanent British settlement.

1789: George Washington becomes the first president of United States of America.

1789–1799: French Revolution.

1793: Execution of Louis XVI; France a republic.

1799: Napoleon becomes first consul and disbands the ruling Directory.

1804: Napoleon crowns himself emperor of France.

1805: British defeat combined Franco-Spanish fleet at Trafalgar.

1807: Slave trade abolished within British empire.

1812: Napoleon's invasion of Russia ends in disaster for him and his army.

1815: British under Wellington and Prussians under Blucher defeat **Napoleon** at battle of Waterloo. **Napoleon** exiled to St. Helena.

1818: Shaka forms Zulu nation in southern Africa.

1819: Singapore founded by British as a base for East India Company.

1821–1829: Greek War of Independence against Turkey.

1822: Brazil becomes independent from Portugal. State of Great Columbia (Venezuela, Colombia, Ecuador, and Panama) set up under Simón Bolívar; becomes independent from Spain.

1825: First passenger steam railroad opens in England.

1835–1837: Great Trek when Boers leave Cape Colony in South Africa and found the state of Transvaal.

1837–1901: Reign of **Queen Victoria** of Great Britain.

1845: Texas and Florida become states of the U.S.

1848: Year of revolutions, including Paris, Milan, Naples, Venice, Rome, Berlin, Vienna, Prague, and Budapest. **Marx** and Engels issue *Communist Manifesto*. California gold rush.

1853: Gold rush in Australia.

1854: Perry forces Japanese to sign treaty agreeing to trade with U.S.

1854–1856: Crimean War; Britain, France and Turkey against Russia.

1857–1858: Indian Mutiny.

1861–1865: American Civil War.

1861: Unification of Italy.

1863: Slavery abolished in U.S.

1866: Prussia defeats Austria and wins leadership of Germany.

1867: U.S. buys Alaska from Russia. Canada becomes British dominion.

1870–1871: Franco-Prussian War.

1871: Germany united; Wilhelm I, king of Prussia, becomes first emperor.

1880–1881: First Boer War between Britain and Dutch settlers (Boers) in Transvaal, South Africa.

1886: Gold discovered in Transvaal; Johannesburg founded.

1890: Wounded Knee, last Native American uprising in U.S.

1897: Pierre and Marie Curie discover radioactive element, radium.

1898: Spanish-American war. U.S. seizes Philippines, Guam, and Puerto Rico.

1899–1902: Second Boer War.

1901: Commonwealth of Australia established.

1903: In U.S. Wright brothers make first powered aircraft flight.

1904–1905: Japan and Russia at war; Japan victorious.

1907: New Zealand becomes British dominion.

1910: Union of South Africa established as British dominion.

1911: Revolution in China. Sun Yat-Sen leads new Chinese republic (1912). Norwegian explorer Roald Amundsen first to reach South Pole.

1912: Henry Ford begins mass production of automobiles in U.S.

1914–1918: World War I.

1917: Russian Revolution.

1919: Peace treaty of Versailles signed.

1920: League of Nations founded.

1922: **Mussolini** comes to power in Italy. Irish Free State proclaimed. Union of Soviet Socialist Republics (U.S.S.R.) founded.

1924: **Lenin** dies; **Stalin** becomes dictator of Russia in 1927.

1927: Charles Lindbergh makes first solo flight across the Atlantic. Civil war in China after Chiang Kai-shek breaks with Chinese communists.

1929: Wall Street crash begins world-wide recession. In India, **Gandhi** begins campaign of civil disobedience against British.

1933: **Hitler** becomes German chancellor; becomes *Führer* (leader) and dictator (1934). U.S. president Roosevelt introduces New Deal policy to end American depression.

1934–1935: Mao Zedong leads the Long March of Chinese communists in northern China; establishes him as leader of Chinese communist party.

1935: Nazis enact anti-Semitic laws in Germany. Italy invades Ethiopia.

1936–1939: Spanish Civil War.

1937: Japanese invade China.

1939: Germany invades Poland.

1939–1945: World War II.

1945: U.S. drops atom bombs on Hiroshima and Nagasaki. United Nations formed.

1946: Indochina: War between Vietnamese nationalists and French.

1947: India and Pakistan become independent. U.S. aid speeds recovery of Europe (Marshall Plan).

1948: U.S.S.R. blockades Berlin; the Berlin airlift. State of Israel declared. Arabs at war with Israel.

1949: NATO formed. Germany becomes two republics, East and West. **Mao Zedong** establishes communist rule in China. Apartheid laws introduced in South Africa.

1950–1953: Korean War: N. Korea and China against S. Korea, the U.S. and UN troops. U.S. tests hydrogen bomb.

1953: Death of **Stalin**. Tito becomes president of Yugoslavia (until 1980).

1954: French leave Vietnam; Vietnam becomes two states, North (communist) and South.

1954–1962: Algerian war between France and Algerian nationalists.

1955: Communist states in East Europe sign Warsaw Pact.

1956: Britain and France, with Israeli help, fail to take control of Suez Canal, nationalized by Egypt's President Nasser.

1957: Treaty of Rome establishes European Common Market. Ghana (Gold Coast) becomes first British African colony to win independence.

1960: Africa: 17 former French and British colonies become independent.

1961: Berlin Wall built.

1962: Cuban Missile Crisis. Algeria becomes independent from France.

1963: President **Kennedy** assassinated.

1964–1975: Vietnam War: civil war with U.S. forces supporting South Vietnam; ends with victory of communist North Vietnam.

1967: Six Day Arab-Israeli War.

1969: American Neil Armstrong first human on Moon. Violence between Protestant majority and Catholic minority in Northern Ireland (Ulster) brings British troops from mainland.

1971: East Pakistan becomes Bangladesh.

1973: Britain, Denmark, and Irish Republic join EC. Israel defeats Arab states in Yom Kippur war.

1979: Israel and Egypt sign peace treaty.

1982: Argentina occupies Falkland Islands. Driven out by British troops.

1985–1991: Mikhail Gorbachev becomes leader of U.S.S.R.

1988: Gorbachev begins reforms in U.S.S.R.—restructuring (*perestroika*) and openness (*glasnost*).

1989: Communist governments in East Germany, Poland, Romania, Bulgaria, and Czechoslovakia overthrown by popular uprisings. Dismantling of Berlin Wall.

1990: Unification of Germany. Iraq invades Kuwait.

1991: The Gulf War—UN forces liberate Kuwait. Civil war begins in Yugoslavia. Apartheid laws in South Africa begin to be dismantled. Boris Yeltsin first democratically elected president of Russia.

1992: South African whites vote to negotiate end of white minority rule. Czechoslovakia moves toward separate Czech and Slovak states.

1993: Italian government reforms following Mafia corruption.

INDEX

Page numbers in *italic* type refer to illustrations.

Page numbers in **bold** type refer to key topics

A

Aborigines *64, 65*
Acre *26, 27,* 86
Acropolis *17*
Africa:
European colonies 68–69
famines 82, *82*
independence 80, 81, 88
slave trade 30, **44–45,** *44–45,* 87, 88
Age of Reason 48–49, *48–49*
   see also Enlightenment
Aircraft *70, 73, 74*
Akbar, Emperor *38,* 84, 88
Alaric *20,* 86
Alexander the Great 16, 84, 86
Algeria *80,* 88
American Civil War 62–63
American Revolution 52–53,
   52–53
Americas 30, **34–35,** 37, **40–41,** *42, 42,*
   44, 86, 87, 88
   see also North America; South
      America; United States of America
Amphitheaters *18*
Anasazi *34,* 86
Angola *45,* 81
Apartheid 83, 88
Arabs 24, 25, 44, *81,* 86, 87, 88
Arawaks 37, 40
Archaeologists 10, *10*
Architecture 31, *48*
Armada *33*
Armor 21, *21, 27, 27*
Army, Roman *20–21*
Art 31, *48, 78, 79*
Arthur, King *23*
Asia 38–39
   communism 76
   European colonies 51, 68
   independence 80
   World War II *74*
Asoka, Emperor 15
Assyrians *13,* 86
Atahualpa *40*
Athens 16, *17*
Atomic bombs 75, 88
Attila 84, 86
Augustus, Emperor 18, 20, 84, 86
Australia 37, *64, 64,* 65, 87, 88
Australopithecines *10*
Austria *70, 71*
Axis Powers 74
Aztecs 34, *34, 40,* 86, 87

B

Babar *38,* 84, 87
Babylonians *13,* 86
Bach, Johann Sebastian *49,* 84
Bahamas 34, 36
Balkans *38, 71*
Ballet 48, *48*
Bangladesh *82,* 88
Baroque art *48,* 85
Bastille *54, 55*
Baths, Roman *19*
Bayeux Tapestry *23*
Beatles 79
Beethoven, Ludwig van 84
Beijing *39, 69,* 77
Belgian Congo (now Zaire) 81
Belgium 59, 60, 61, 70
Bengal *51*
Benin empire *44,* 86
Berlin Wall 76, 82, *83,* 88
Bible, The 15
Bismarck, Otto von 84
Black Death 28–29, *29,* 86
Black Hole of Calcutta 51
Boleyn, Anne 33
Bolívar, Simón 61, 84
Bolivia 61
Boston Tea Party 52
Bows and arrows *28, 35*
Boyars 46
Brazil 40, *45, 51,* 88
Britain:
   British empire 41, 50, 68–69, *68,* 80, *80*
   Civil War 46, *47,* 87
   Hundred Years' War 28
   Industrial Revolution *58–59, 58–59*
   Napoleonic wars 56, 57
   nuclear power 83
   Reformation in *32,* 33
   slave trade 45
   theaters *42, 43*
   World War I 70
   World War II 74, *74–75*
Britain, Battle of 75
Bruegel, Peter 31
Brunelleschi, Filippo 31
Buddhism 14, 15, *15,* 84, 86
Bunker Hill, battle of *53*
Byzantine empire 21, 38, 86, 87

C

Cabot, John 37, 87
Cabral, Pedro 40
California 65
Calvin, John 32, 33, 87

Canada 41, 65, 87, 88
Canals *58*
Cape of Good Hope 40, *50,* 87
Caravels *36*

Carpaccio, Vittore 31, *31*
Carthaginians 18
Castles 26, *28*
Castro, Fidel 77, 84
Catherine of Aragon 33
Catherine the Great 84, 87
Catholic Church 32–33, 39, 49, 69
Cave paintings *11*
Caxton, William 31, 87
Centurion, HMS 51
Champlain, Samuel de *50*
Chaplin, Charlie 73, *73*
Charlemagne 84, 86
Charles I, king of England 46, *47,* 84,
   87
Charles II, king of England *44,* 46,
   49
Charles VII, king of France *28*
Charles X, king of France 61
Chernobyl 82
Chiang Kai-shek 77, 84
Child labor *59*
Chile 61
China 38–39, 86, 88
   communism in 76, 77, 88
   Marco Polo visits 37, 38
   Han dynasty 86
   Ming dynasty *39*
   Opium wars 69
   religions 14, 15, *15,* 86
Chivalry 27
Christianity 14, **24**
   Crusades *26–27*
   in Middle Ages 22
   missionaries 49, 69
   Reformation **32–33,** 87
   in Roman empire 21, 86
   Victorian Age 66
Church of England 33
Churchill, Sir Winston 84
Circus Maximus 18, *18*

89

The publishers would like to thank the following artists
for contributing to the book:

Jonathan Adams 47, 54, 58–59, 61, 72–73, 77;
Marion Appleton 10–11, 12, 15, 18–19, 21, 22–23, 25, 27, 29, 31, 34, 36, 38–39, 44, 47, 48–49, 59, 79, 83;
Vanessa Card 24; Dean Entwistle 12–13, 18–19, 24–25; Eugene Fleury maps, various pages;
Mark Franklin maps, various pages; Terry Gabbey (EVA Morris AFA) 10–11,
14–15, 31;
Peter Gregory 35, 78–79, 80; Andre Hrydziusko (Simon Girling) 26, 31;
Simon Huson 10;
Ron Jobson (Kathy Jakeman Illustration) 22, 27, 33, 36, 59, 67, 74;
Kevin Jones Associates 32, 35, 39, 40, 45, 59, 73, 76–77;
Peter Kestervan (Garden Studio) 19, 24, 36, 62–63, 70–71;
Deborah Kindred (Simon Girling) 23, 25, 29, 30, 41;
Mike Lacey (Simon Girling) 28, 56–57, 72; Jason Lewis 43; Chris Lyon 75;
Louis Mackay (Linda Rogers) 30, 42;
Dave McAllister (Simon Girling) 13, 20–21, 26–27, 40–41, 52–53, 68–69;
Tony Morris (Linda Rogers) 49, 54, 65, 78; Trevor Parkin (Linda Rogers) 43, 45;
Mike Roffe 51; Martin Salisbury (Linda Rogers) 43, 60, 73, 79, 83;
Rodney Shackell 33, 43, 45, 48–49, 55, 60–61, 62, 64, 67; Rob Shone 25, 66;
Nick Shewring 73; Paul Stangroom 30, 32–33, 55, 60, 62, 82;
Roger Stewart 50–51, 54, 66, 67; Graham Sumner (Simon Girling) 46–47, 52–53, 64, 80;
Mike Taylor 59

The publishers would like to thank the following for supplying
photographs for this book:

Frontispiece AKG; page 16–17 SCALA; 18 AKG; 23 Permission of Town of Bayeux;
25 ZEFA; 27 British Museum; 28 British Library (top), Bridgeman Art Library
(bottom); 31 AKG; 34 British Museum; 35 British Museum; 38 AKG; 39 British
Museum; 42 Science Museum; 43 Bridgeman Art Library; 48 AKG; 52 Peter Newark
Pictures (left), Library of Congress (right); 53 Peter Newark Pictures; 57
Bridgeman Art Library; 63 AKG; 65 Mary Evans Picture Library (left),
Bettmann Archive (right); 68 Bridgeman Art Library; 69 National Army Museum;
71 AKG; 72 Bettmann Archive; 74 Imperial War Museum; 75 Wiener Library/Beate
Klarsfeld Foundation (top), Associated Press (middle), Imperial War Museum
(bottom); 77 Popperfoto; 79 Popperfoto (middle), Chatto and Windus (bottom);
80 Hulton-Deutsch Collection; 81 Popperfoto; 82 Frank Spooner Pictures.

(AKG = Archiv Fur Kunst Und Geschichte)